Part ONE

I Allowed Myself to Be...

Come Back, My Son Come Back

Krystyna Napierala

I dedicate this book to every person on the globe.

Everyone is the same most important apple of the eye of the only one eternal God

CONTENTS

PREFACE

I wrote this book with you in my mind.
While reading, you may not agree with me
immediately. That's OK. I can wait.
But I expect that you tell me instantly about any
dissonance; boldly – loudly - precisely.
You will develop a useful skill for life, and you will
be able to compose and hear your protest at the
comfort of your chair.
It is very constructive and healing. Why churn
anything inside yourself?

Yes, check it out how it sounds.
Yes, you have to learn to stand up for yourself.
I can volunteer to be your slope tree and back you
up sometimes for even easier mounting.

At the moment, I can hear that you do not use
the Power of your Authority, which resides in the
tone of your voice.
I can feel that you have been too shy while judging
your potential.
And I can guess that your innate modesty
annihilates your energy to hold you back.
I can see your dreams so restricted that they do
not dare to cross the dream slot.
And I know that your "I AM" is fused with the heart
of God. If you do not understand such an Entity, I
can give you a clue - He is three times OMNI!

This book will impose on your mind your legal POWER, which is so bored and exhausted of being a dormant companion with the potential of erupting volcano.
The power of your will should guard you against any invasion; nothing in this whole universe has a legal right to invade you to harm you; even to cross your boundaries like a germ, for example.

You need to exercise your AUTHORITY not only over your life but also over your body. Everything in you must stay in perfect shape and health - just command – and admire my last example.
After my whole life in lethargy, I am progressing with energy - only this tiny cluster of muscles which chew the food refused to act just recently. My weakness for food has been overpowered by disempowering eating machine!
I am shaking with laughter at my new disability while losing my fat; no pain in the cheeks while giggling. I also noticed that the Divine deals with problems in the same mood as your tone of attunment. Even imperative obligations can be resolved in a joke-like style; lightly and smoothly.

Remember to be patient, that restoration will take some time. Not in a moment, one can get back on the designed track; you used the whole life to make it so bad.

Yet, you should be aware that there is the Legal
Right to say "Noooo!" to anything which you do not
fancy and lies within the field of personal choice.
I closed all the windows and doors to express that
newly gained wisdom, and I am here now,
finishing my book. I couldn't grab the pen for over
sixty years, as a tiny child I chose the titles.
To the other staff of global influence, you can only
add your protest. But get your voice heard if only
to feel good within yourself. What you cannot cope
with, bless it and pass on God - and He will be
delighted to participate.

You are always attached to Him by the ribbon of
Light and Love, and it is called Angel. God is more
than happy to participate actively in your life. He
"launched" you to Earth for that purpose only; to
be in you and create through you. Imagine how
God must be fed up with the speed and perfection
of his process of creation; a thought - a word –
bum, it's done!
You see, God wants it a bit slower, awkwardly,
and with errors - to have more space for the
enjoyment of the do-ing process until He is ready
to pat you on your back, "Well done Bob, Great
Job, It was such a delight to take part in that
show!" God wants you to exercise perseverance,
obedience, respect to physical laws, patience.

Give God such luxury and warmth in the area of your Temple.

Thus, you must admit that you and I have to combine our efforts, fire it with curiosity to elicit hidden gifts and talents, to explore in us more than we dared to dream so far. I will back you up - you will ensure me that I was right.
Then you can close your eyes to see whom to invite to help with a more fabulous project; rather avoid managing only by yourself.

I received the gift of Prophecy 55 years ago - at first, I was frightened, and I did not know what to do with it.
Sometimes, under intense inner pressure, I opened my mouth to tell something. It occurred to be authentic, indeed.
Sometimes I withdrew the urge – only to regret: Oh, what if I dared to speak, to predict, what a hero I could have become!

Just recently, I learned that I could prophesy actively, i.e. to create predictions myself. In my exact circumstances, I am the one who feels strong the needs at the very moment in that environment. Thus my spoken word is a command to God's force to locate the result which will rescue, restore, deliver something directly to this site.

I could have help people and many impersonal situations, yet such a gift from God I kept dormant for so long.

Nevertheless, after studying this issue in-depth, I have learned that every one of us has such a duty to prophesy. You must utter your plans to induce the vibration in the universe, to combine the most intriguing network of delivery. Proclaim your prophecy as a ceremony; it will be easier to remember, keep you alert, and expect the shipment.
Because if you choose from the point of respecting the highest good - you are like God at that current moment of need. You may be an atheist, yet your spoken word will have the power of manifesting whenever the needs align with the will of God.
Your word will sound like a Decree which God can act out only through you at that place and moment.
God resides in your heart, whether you wish or not.
Yet, by the power of your will, you can silence God within - think how to use your willpower wiser.

Remember to prophesy always for a good reason and goal - only for a higher purpose and intent.
I have just Prophesied that the very process of reading this book will empower every reader – his mind refreshed - her mindset changed.

Continue, even if you feel tired now. It is your first step to empower your will to stretch out your perseverance. I will insert in this book a lot of know-how secrets on the topic of wellbeing – they gave me a chance to exist, to be and deal with most significant events, although feeling debilitating lack of energy and pain.
Whatever I write, I do not aim to change your creed; I only suggest you better attune to God who resides in you and then feel free to think and keep the mind open. I failed to take that advantage for most of my years; my life could have been more natural.

God volunteered to be massacred for you - to grant you the right to spectacular life and then to Eternity – for you, regardless of your disbelief, disrespect for God and anything affected by Love. Do not despair about any failure, bless it and wash away with Divine blood. Listen to your inspiration; act when the idea and time feel right. Any discomfort, pain, trouble pass on God if you cannot cope.
With God in your heart, you will always feel secure and be on the right path.

I am creating a Blog so as we can exchange our experience once we crushed our limitations - any comments from you will nourish the community. Look for details in the link - Like the

Page to receive updates and see the video with advice how to boost energy and memory – my new secret helped me rapidly; I can write books!

https://www.facebook.com/IAllowedMyselfToBe

FOREWORD

My name is Amb. Dr JOYCE FRANCIS from India;
the same name on Facebook.
I am writing from the core of my heart and would
like you to read and know my thinking about the
efforts that Krystyna has done.
It was so engaging and thoughtful that I got glued
to it, and it forced me to think a couple of things. In
other words, the benefits that a person is going to
acquire not only reading it once but making it as a
habit on a daily note.

Thank you, Krystyna, for the effort & planning to
write and elaborate in such an excellent way which
brings us closer to God – the source of Wisdom,
Hope, Freedom, Lasting Joy.
This book gave me a different vision of God and
my role as a human being in this world. People
indeed should find pleasure in caring for others. I
read only half of the book, as Krystyna keeps
writing the rest. This writing empowers me even
more to continue my charity work.

As you may find out, I am trying to manage &
run a non-profit charity NGO called MERLE
REBIRTH ORGANISATION in the state of
Jharkhand, India from the past couple of years.
Due to the Internet, the world has become smaller.
We may never meet, but the Faith in God is what

brings us together and close to each other, and helps us to help others.

Amb. Dr Joyce Francis, India, Jharkhand

I just finished reading this book and can't believe that my friend from Facebook could write all that; I admire such talent for writing and expressing yourself.

I loved it, found it absorbing, and as a Christian, it all made sense to me. The intriguing part was that as a child, Krystyna knew straight away that she wanted to share her knowledge with everyone else, and she is doing that by writing this captivating book.
Good luck to you. I will certainly buy this book when it comes out, and I look forward to reading every one. Well done, Krystyna!

Barbara Lucas, UK, Retired Partner from John Lewis retailer

I am Naeem Akbar Dar hailing from Pakistan, a Lawyer and an employee of Public Organization in Islamabad. I'm a writer of some historical books.

I have gone through the half of the book as the author still writes, and it gave me immense pleasure that Krystyna Napierala has attempted such a sensitive issue, which contains excellent knowledge.
This particular book is unique since it covers the wealth of information; the distillation of knowledge from luminaries, reflecting the multiethnic background of the philosophical notions which I believe are very crucial/essential to humankind to discern.
While going through the book, the author's dogmatic views about the equality of man gives me an insight of looking at human nature adversely. It has enlightened my understandings of God.

This masterpiece of literature has exquisitely woven the relationship between men and God, and such endeavour is evident and uplifting. When we employ a subtler intellect, we can re-evolve from the confines of modem science from the evidence-based on dead matter and its properties to revisiting the philosophy of our ancients.

God is omnipotent and eternal, and there is enough of Him to take care of the whole burden of humanity.
The path of sin is sweeter than to move in the upright, ethical and challenging way. Thus to be on the right track, transformation becomes inevitable, and eventually, this suffering pulls us towards eternal light.
Why not invite God into daily life?

God's benevolence is buoyant, which is evident in the case of Jesus / Christ. Books skillfully weaved the catastrophe of crucifixion, which helps me to understand that shortcut to Eternity in Heaven. My comprehensions get clear about the fact that every one of us would go back to God.

The author strongly emphasises that the participation of the Jews in the history of world salvation should be reviewed and corrected. The Jewish elite entailed God's plan of redemption of the world through the crucifixion of Jesus Christ; the Jews fulfilled to the letter Divine intention.

This book has tackled the threads about the subject of love between God and his creation very artistically as God always shows his love through actions. As Love, He sent down Christ, followed by the incident of spilling blood to save humankind.

Love is the core of God's nature, thus is inseparable. However, emotions like hatred, jealousy lead humanity towards destructive consequences. Since it is crystal clear that to err is human, therefore God has designed these feelings, which sustain the fire of life and fuel our actions. Furthermore, the devastating results affect eternal destiny. To bury the hatchet, God guides humankind toward forgiveness and redemption; gives His life on the cross to seal the concept.

The core message, "Once forgiven it becomes automatically forgotten", prevails security, love and peace in life, and spiritual development.
The best thing I find about the book is that it doesn't only address a particular audience; instead, its subjects are beyond gender, caste and creed. This attitude is the dawn of a new era of intellectual cooperation of an international nature where the only boundaries are the limitations of one's thinking.

The author conveys the insight that only our sins turn into a wall which separates a man from God, although God desires to forgive every time.
The publication educates the mind and through every single individual simultaneously empower and unite different religions and nationalities.

This book opens the thoughts process proficiently and negotiates the concept of Spirit of God penetrating a material form for the people of bone and flesh. Views of this book delicately deal with an affinity between a man and God.

I want to congratulate Krystyna for this plausible literacy work which targets all sort of readers but would also serve as a reference book.
This book is a benchmark for publications in this smaller world of the new millennia.

Naeem Akbar Dar, a Friend from Facebook
Lawyer at Public Organization

CHAPTER ONE

INSIGHT INTO THE DIVINE

Be like ME!

Stand up for yourself!

— I Allowed Myself to Be Massacred —

To undo the consequence

I did not give up my position and place!

Have Faith that I will give you full support,

whenever you stand your ground in defence of

righteousness

With such statements, God addressed my accusations
and consoled me in my dramatic situation.

WOW! So nice to be with you!

Now, when we are together, let's overhear this intriguing dialogue:
-"Why did you drop such a black blot on my face?
– Asked a draft of a female.
- It will be the apple within the azure iris of your seducing eyes.
- Oh, I am so glad.

But after a little while, another remark:
- Why my eyes are out of alignment! - The picture was furious, not curious.
- It's so annoying to paint females!" - Picasso dropped his paintbrush.

Sorry, it was me who created this dialogue, to elicit a warning for you;
"You Masterpiece, do not control the Master." I will inject it to you on every occasion!
I intend to compose a few volumes of this Book, but for you – if you dislike reflecting on the core issue of existence – it could be enough to read in-depth only this Insight into the Divine. Many of us speculate that searching in past errors will help design wiser future tomorrow while the current trend suggests to be fully present in the NOW and enjoy life as it comes. I am not afraid to outstand from the crowd and propose you to keep a balance between the three – and aim for the highest level of ETERNITY.

So, even if you are not keen to explore the wonders of Divine complexness, maybe you would read scrupulously only the Insight and skip all the other chapters? Or leave them for later? But promise me that you will endure this smaller task as it took me almost 60 years to grab the pen. May any newly learned idea vibrates in your Being, may it vocalise in your soul song. May it rumble all deliberate blockages you carefully built to distinct your personality while aiming for vanity. Set your goals beyond the horizon of your universe and harvest enough on your trail that you'll never need to be born again.

Whoever you are, whatever is your age and gender;
However high is your social status or a bank statement?
Are you already famous or on the way to your greatness,
Wherever you live, in a remote village or a big city centre,
I wrote this book only for you. You might be the only one who decided to spend some time to explore the subtle side of the Divine world! I hope you will strive to keep your eyes opened even if it is a late night.

That "God does not exist" is a trendy pose for many young people. Also, many adults feel

withdrawn – forgetting that God can only act and repair the world through His people. He continuously calls for attention if you willingly opened the eyes, mind, heart.
I will provide many examples and advice. Read this book in your quiet time and also calm and open your mind to be more receptive, to deepen your understanding.

I am not concerned about the depth of your belief system, how smart you are, your size, or the name of your bank - I witnessed so many changes. I am positive that we are both equal at the soul level, obviously.

I guess in your close circle of friends, everyone says; you are with us in the role of a talisman to charm others into a puzzle of a social network. You are a distinctive dot on the countenance of mother Earth.
Every dot attributes equally to the whole portrait no matter if it builds up a neck or a nail, no matter if the colours of eyes lure us with amazing azure or are the only grey.

You are indeed the same apple in God's eyes, like I. You must be the same gem with unique curves modelled over the time which also sculptured mine. You represent another cell yet of the same divine body of Christ, like me and everybody else. Do you value more a cell in your liver or the brain?

I accept all of the mines equally – wherever they arranged themselves to be. And they function without any need to give thanks; if some of them fail – I start thinking about how to save them. "Give them life," apply a hot water bottle - my common sense would suggest. Heat brings blood to the affected area, "warmth and blood can restore the flesh."

Blood is Life – you can learn from the Bible – thus it must be able to heal almost anything! Hey, wouldn't the same remedy deliver us safely to eternal level? Certainly.

As above so below, the best instructive hint is hidden somewhere in libraries of wisdom. Yet to the other side of human nature, it may whisper – "you are not better than others!" The same concept can put one person in mental paradise, another one in distress!

How often do you reflect over a route throughout your life? Is your path meandering from below to above? Is your current day the same as yesterday - does the likeness happen for the sake of easiness?

Contrary to our tendency to sameness as a recipe, God's creativity is unlimited. Nothing exists in the same state along the chain of change –

even if something looks similar or repeats itself. I would often be satisfied with the sameness in the human sense - to be solely the best like everybody else; the most beloved, the only unique apple. It is comforting to know that God has this ability to treat everyone as if you were the same and the Only One as well. I heard it from eye-witnesses who came back after death, or from visitations to Heaven.

Progress in science makes it easy to explain; notice how Google tries to resemble God. No matter how many millions computer addicts search for bread giving ideas or entertainment, or are just curious, Google deals with every request within a second as if you were the Only One user.

Let's meet the Divine

Your success is God's desire for you felt with the same intensity of the driving force – and then He desires that after your earthly mission, your horses will drive you back home to Him. You can appear indebted; you can come empty-handed like the prodigal son. Yet as you are coming dressed in His uniform – He will recognise you like the most splendour Knight - because you will wear the heartfelt scarlet scarf made of Jesus' Blood; Divine Blood.

Your gracious image will indicate that you have sacrificed at least a second of your life to regret and ask God for forgiveness – and then pleaded His precious Blood to wash away your sins. Something in my style - Dear Dad, I regret that I have sinned, please forgive me, wash away my guilt with your precious Blood.
Or, say – I plead your Blood for my sins. Or, even better, invent your personal version. God prefers if you speak to Him in your heart. He is there in awaiting state, and you need to invite Him to act.

And that would be enough to secure happiness for eternity even if you made such declaration in your thoughts only, even if simultaneously with your last breath. Just have faith that you will enjoy the eternity in God's abundance and await the perfection of all goodness.
In the affinity of Faith lies the assurance that you will always be observant about:
HOW DO YOU WANT TO SPEND ETERNITY?
WHERE DO YOU WANT TO SPEND ETERNITY?

What about those who deny God?
I, and many others, volunteer in praying to Father God and Jesus on their behalf. Yet, I am not sure if my saying for them, "I AM sorry, Dad" will count

the same. Every one of us has the same limitation;
no one can utter I AM for another person. "I AM" is
your unique sound to declare your dominion,
authority and power in every provocation.

    Please remember, whoever you are, wherever
you live, whatever your belief – do not consider
Jesus as Religion – He is God who loves every
goodness taught by every religion.
He used to live on earth for a while to accomplish
many goals, colossal in importance. Before He
died, He had promised to come back soon.
And it has to come that this is happening now.
I saw Jesus in the sky as big as the firmament.
It is one of the reassuring signs, as he had
declared.
I have to write speedily to spread this most
fantastic news. If Jesus comes back now, it can
only mean that humanity needs imminent rescue
from this catastrophic environment.
 Your liver cannot remove your whole meal as
toxins, and your lungs don't know how to reject the
air you breathe.

    When Jesus lived with us, and it is a historical
fact, He was ready to help every person in
distress. Then He promised to build up mansions
in Heavenly cities; most probably only one for
everyone.
And the new place is much more superior than the

paradise designed by Father God to His first people.
Can I have the full attention of all your ears? I am going to whisper to you the most enjoyable secret. No one noticed any mysterious trees bearing forbidden fruits in the heavenly environment. I will write in other chapters reports from many visitors to Heaven who were invited by Jesus or Father God. Even on YouTube, you can find a lot.

The little golden key to enter your mansion you will find in your heart; Father God or Jesus will hold it in His palm. But you need to give them the right to act in your space. Just ask Jesus or God: Be my Lord or Be the Lord of my heart.

Remember not to identify Jesus with any religion; He is all for everyone - God in the flesh, one with the Father God in Spirit.
You are not a stranger to Jesus; He holds your purpose for your life in His finger-tip, guiding you quietly to make the correct imprint. You can find your name as if carved in the palm of His hand – He cannot remove you from His consciousness.

Alchemy of the Word

   I distinguish Jesus as God in the flesh for the creation from the matter.
God The Father exists in Spirit form. Through Jesus, every God's thought turns into the Word. God's Light splits into colours... God's Love breaks into elements... thus even dust carry Love and Jesus considered it as a suitable matter for the creation of Adam.

   Will God allow a human to dig down into alchemy of His Word?
Let's ponder on the human one first. A word consists of a sequence of sounds or written letters.

To create a word - human must have practised how to use voice. The sounds spoken in a particular sequence - through letters turn into material existence. Both words, spoken or written, produce the same meaning, which instantly can turn into a vision or feeling.
The latter directly can stir your state of being.

 Yet nothing material so far.
Although there is no matter, no sound, no vision at first - how come that you can write down your thoughts straight from your head!
Libraries collect written words imprisoned in books; inside the walls, there is a universe of

compressed meanings and feelings. Luckily hidden words cannot express anything, and you are safe to enter such buildings.

In God's Spirituality, there must exist a potential to create and relate to the material world in our material Universe. From God's heart, the ideas flow out as Love and Jesus transform every one of them into a visible image.

The Divine Trinity coexist and governs this Universe; in other universes, God may exist as another concept beyond the human possibility of comprehension by our limited mind and senses.

For simple understanding; Jesus and Father God can be separate - but equal. They can be united - blend into One Energy of Light and Love. When Jesus sits on the right side of the Throne, the Throne itself is not separable. Jesus said many times, "My Father and I are one." This information lingers throughout the Holy Bible. I received from God 3-hearted plant, and the unusual change of heart's identity simplifies the understanding of the Trinity - I will present it in further chapters.

For now, let's speed up with this Chapter to spread the good news. Rejoice the Earth - Jesus is coming back. When? Now!
Such glory is going to affect our life now - I saw a huge picture of Jesus across the whole sky.

The way to the Cross

God Jesus lived on earth two thousand years ago, born into the Jewish community as the Son of God. Jesus was not recognised in his role to assure that the purpose of His mission would succeed.

God-Jesus was born into his chosen nation to live in the flesh as a human to become their Messiah. The core of the plan was to challenge satanic forces into the plot of taking His life. The most important and secret idea was that the shed of the blood on the cross would have to be the cause of death.
Having this goal on the mind, Jesus diplomatically kept moving ahead towards the destiny on the cross. He never said words of appreciation to Pharisees, chief priests, scribes. Like a crazy man, Jesus chastised merchants with a hand-made whip! But notice that Jesus chased them away from the same Temple which He had attended earlier on many occasions.

At the very end, that man known locally as the son of Joseph revealed that He was the Son of God. To anyone's dismay, the popular idol started to suggest madly and repetitively that only through consuming his blood and flesh, a person would be able to enter Heaven after death!

To many of the listeners, it meant the end of their hopes and their world. Many from them intended to stone Jesus to death on the spot. Such a shame, such disappointment, so much time wasted on his lecturing...
At that time it became clear for the public what was the source of the previous magical tricks. At last, Jesus exposed to people His real state of consciousness. Whoever could hear His latest announcement, could add negative gossips about the famous one who raised Lazarus from the dead; a decomposed body of a man.
 Bad and good rumours twittered from mouth to mouth.

   It is so easy to filter the news and explain doubts after facts; it is so easy to acknowledge the symbol of bread and wine, which are so obvious now, but...
Position yourself at that place, become a member of the crowd and try to understand these declarations as they sound. How would you digest their literal meaning?
When Jesus said, "My Father and I are One" (John 10:30-31) - then the mob picked up stones again to stone Him. In such moment, most probably the members of the public expressed their anger, not chief priests or scribes.

Political background

The latest public blasphemy by the son of local carpenter Joseph, about being the Son of God, offering to eat his flesh and drinking his blood... That was too much for the ears of any average person.
Whatever popularity Jesus had gained, all vanished, and the mood of the crowd turned into anger.

It enraged all the Jewish authorities – but what's more – endangered Jews as a nation staying under Roman occupation.
Jesus had already bewitched the majority of the population; people cried out: The King of Israel!
The Jew elite had to act: "better if One dies to rescue all of us."

Alas, if the world would recognise their brilliant mind!
If we all could realise that Jews were saying the most dramatic truth for the whole of humankind.
But Jesus was not in the position to glorify them and say, "You must be inspired", when chief priests and the crowd yelled during prosecution, "Nail him to the cross", Cesar is our King!"

Now, Pontius Pilate was in real trouble; he received a warning from his wife to safe Jesus. On

the other hand, the Rulers could question Pilate's
political loyalty.
Thus, that purely political background became the
cornerstone for Pontius to sentence Jesus to
death, as indicates the guilt – I.N.R.I. - which
meant: 'Jesus of Nazareth, King of the Jews'.
Such was the statement of guilt; Pontius Pilate
ordained to write over the head of Jesus when the
soldiers nailed Jesus to the cross.

Only the intellectual, spiritual cream of the
Jewish nation could have arranged such a twist of
fate for the freshly acclaimed King of Israel. If it
reached Cesar's ear that people were spreading
their garments and leafy brunches on the road
shouting Hosanna to King of Israel!
And to whom! To a suspicious young man riding
on a small colt!

Herod heard rumours about the man's some
magical skills, but people were also saying that the
man was out of his mind, that he was saying
things which would turn out not only the stomach
but also everyone's ability to judge.
"They have never greeted me like this" – would
think any Ruler, growing natural hatred towards
waving population.
Romans would never tolerate the desire for Israel
to become the blessed kingdom of David. "Crash
the evil in the bud" action would follow, which

meant political regime, restrictions, the possibility of genocide.

Upon the birth of Jesus, astronomers had read in the stars that a King came to the world. In consequence, all boys under two years of age lost their lives.

The Jews complete God's Plan

Undoubtedly, everyone in the population remembered the fate of those baby-boys, killed when news about newly born King reached Herod's ears. This time the Jewish authorities tried to prevent genocide; their decision seemed to be justified to sacrifice ONE person to save the whole nation.

History still hides that God used his chosen nation to save all countries from the clutches of Satan. I cannot stress more - this pervasive and entangled chain of events leading to the crucifixion of Jesus could not have been performed better than by the group of Jewish intelligence.
There was absolute alignment with God's desire about His Son's mission: to glorify Jesus as Mediator of a New Covenant and establish the

potential of His precious Blood to wash away sins of every person and Redeem all Nations.

Jewish reasoning; "Sacrifice ONE person to save all of us" perfectly combined the rescue for you and me, for all who lived, and all these to be born. In one word - for the whole world!
Assuredly God will forgive me in this only case if I say first; God, Bless the Jews, and then, Praise the Lord.
What a shame that the world accused Jews of killing their Messiah and this curse still prevails! Already Isaiah had prophesied about blind eyes and hardened hearts imposed on the accusers. We must understand that Jesus had to enrage Pharisees, scribers, chief priest to safeguard God's plan of redemption. Jesus was about to fulfil the role of the Passover Lamb. For that purpose, the Crucifixion had to happen during those next days – or a year later.

Just before the arrest and prosecution, Jesus took all sins of the world on Himself. Thus devils had the legal right to join the scene and then developed cruelty beyond Jews expectations. The Jews elite must have felt guilty and ashamed for the whole procedure of ending the life of the One – the member of their nation - or the strip and strips

during operation of the justice system carried on
by Romans and fuelled by demons!
Neither bankers nor bakers, barbers, builders,
butchers could engage Rulers of occupied
Jerusalem to give death verdict to a highly popular
Jew during festive mood of imminent Passover,
which was the most important national festival for
every person.

In the end, the Pontius Pilate cleared himself
from the guilt of the death sentence, "it was not my
decision, I am not to blame" and he performed
symbolic manifestation of innocence while
washing his hands. There were only Pharisees
and chief priests, and high priest Caiaphas left to
absorb the guilt for that plot of Crucifixion – next
rumour about Resurrection must have put them in
an inner state of hell.

As in a Greek tragedy, let's one part of chores
shout the comments:
- Only the intellectual, spiritual cream of the Jewish
nation could have arranged such a twist of fate for
the freshly acclaimed King of Israel. If it reached
Cesar's ear that occupied population were
spreading their garments and leafy brunches on
the road shouting Hosanna to King of Israel.
And the other part may sing
- High time that guilt and shame of the Jewish elite
be washed away for destroying their own Messiah.

It seems obvious to understand that God used
His beloved Nation as a blind and hard force to
succeed with His genius plan - to liberate the
whole world from the destruction of Satan.
This innocent death opened your gate to eternal
life, can annihilate all wrongdoing which altogether
a tiny word "sins" can congest! What a glory of
achievement!

God's LIFE for Life of All Creation!

The precious Blood pays the devil all your loans
and personal bills for living outside of the
commandments of God, out of the universal legal
system which violates the proverbial common
sense!
The bloodshed also pays for your frequent and
secret choices you are making daily which
disagree with your inner value and intelligence. It
can even pay for moral debt left by your Fathers
and purify the whole Bloodline!
What a glory of achievement; the Heavenly Father
has gained all legal rights to gather all His fallen
children back.

What a joy of the Shepherd not to let down His
sheep!
What a Glory and Peace in the whole Heaven!
What glory should have fallen on the Jews!

What a combined achievement by the nation and their Messiach!

Even God may not know the outcome of His plans before facts; will it work if the Earth is a Free Will paradise?

Even in the Divine circle, there must have been tension:
- if only could it happen that Jesus would die...
- if only for that aim would it be possible to blind all participants...
- if only Jesus as a man could withstand that horror; what if He collapsed and died sooner!

In the free-will zone, nothing is engraved in the stone. There was uncertainty that all combined forces would follow God's plan and destroy the Son of God in the precise time, just in time.
That Jesus would die shortly after nailing to the cross – proving that the death naturally followed the loss of blood as the absolute cause. Just in time to be buried before the Passover.

Only the Blood was so essential for REDEMPTION in universal legal terms because of the Blood association with Life.
"Until heaven and earth pass away, not a single iota or line will change in the law, until all will be fulfilled" [Matt. 5:18].
Life for Life satisfy the Heavenly bill, the scales of

justice are balanced - no arguments, no doubts for
an accuser and the judge.
YES, the whole genius Divine plan has been
fulfilled to the letter.

Who caused that execution of the plan for your
benefit? Who crowned the fulfilment of the rescue
project for you and me?

- The Jews.

Now, remember; I have passed this knowledge
only to you.
Keep it for yourself or share this secret with others
- it would be worth to let your close friends know
and benefit from the Law of Gratitude wherever
they bless a passer-by, Jew.

Yet, Jews are accused

The accusation of Jews for the death of Jesus
probably pushed the whole nation in shame of guilt
and helped to spread the consciousness of anti-
Semitism, and separation.

It must feel like a crust over the injured body,
although Jesus forgave everyone already from the
Cross.
However, it was in the competence of the early

church to reach out their hands and shake with Jews.
"You killed Him" still vibrates in the human consciousness until current time!

As a child, I wanted to shout! What a paradox! What a shame!

During the last 2000 years, there should have been enough brainy leaders to say: God desired that His Son Jesus, born as a Jew , would die on the cross for all humanity to Save and Restore and Deliver - which is the meaning of Jesus as the name in Hebrew.

Jesus skillfully controlled the state of consciousness leading to quick accusation and crucifixion.
The Messiah had to be degraded to the level of an average man so as to become guilty of presenting a false identity as the Son of God.
The Jews authorities hardened their belief that JESUS WASN'T that person they had expected to come, "Jesus was not our Messiah!" And they were truly not conscious of the real role of Jesus – it would have destroyed God's plans.

Thank God "All went well!". Jesus with the Jewish Nation under occupation saved the world – everyone should know. Precious Divine Blood stays with humankind to purify, to heal, to help with anything if applied in Faith by any believer in Jesus as the Saviour of the world.

It was God's Blood flowing in Jesus' veins; Jesus came to Earth only for that purpose; to shed that Blood during the crucifixion – for every person in any Religion. Jesus is above all Religions, Jesus is unified with God. I keep repeating my statements because I am terrified what news I have just read, which have been spread over internet. The top minds still searching, digging, focusing who is guilty, whom to blame! Let's employ gratitude; if not for the Jews, we would not have Redemption, no Xmas, no Easter.

However, we should become aware that the current state of affairs proves the power of the ruler of this darkened world — the Enemy called Satan.
Nowadays, even the statement about the existence of God may end up in a raised tone, or a question mark in written words!
The battle between the Light and dark is going on. Any sin can separate a man from God.

The implied guilt for the crucifixion and the shame, as the worst sin, caused the separation between Jews and Jesus until now – the time of the second coming of the Christ. In a dream, I saw Jesus as big as the whole sky. Let's stop worrying about Jews; Jesus will find a way to unify with God's people.

 Jesus saved them all during the Messiah's first visitation. Would you accept more wonders?

    Hard to comprehend but only the Jews were "saved" in the result of God's Son Crucifixion. Don't try to rebel! I agree with you!

Nevertheless, I will dare to add that that Redemption of Jews extends over all their newly-born until the end of this world.
Do they know it?
- No. Not yet. The Jews are even not aware of anything.
But what about you?

Have you pondered over HOW DO YOU WANT TO SPEND YOUR ETERNITY?

Have you decided WHERE DO YOU WANT TO SPEND YOUR ETERNITY?

You can choose now when you can still decide.
You can decide now while you are still alive.

Concept of Justice

Let me warn you. You are merely a Masterpiece, brace yourself, do not try to rebel against your Master. May the perception of your justice not override your common sense, your position on Earth, your emotions.

You'd better bless every Jew whenever you have a chance. Stay calm and listen to my whisper! The Salvation/the Redemption is infused into Jewish existing belief system.

Neither do they need to know how to win eternity in heaven – nor to claim any benefits of Jesus' sacrifice. All profits fell on them as if by surprise. -Is it not a paradox?

Surely, if I told you that they do not need to believe in Jesus at all?
- What a puzzle!

Yes! And what a surprise Jesus holds for Jews at the gate to heaven ? With overstretched arms like on the Cross, He will joyfully embrace every approaching Jew to pull them through the gate; at the moment when any of them will have passed away.

Nonetheless, do not feel upset about these symptoms of injustice. As you know, all the nations

can benefit from Redemption - you only need to
have FAITH.

All you have to do is to become the Believer of
Jesus as your personal Saviour. And then
continue to worship the only God according to your
religion.
Almost everyone admits that there is the only-one
eternal Almighty God. There are hundreds of
God's names all over the globe; people have a
problem indeed – they cannot compromise on the
name. "*God is God, and God is His name, and He
doesn't need any other one*" – as a tiny girl, I cried
and shouted at my uncle Helbik, whenever he
insisted that the name is Jehovah!

I am writing this book urgently to put the end of
this historical conflict and confusion. All the people
have to acknowledge;
- God allowed Himself voluntarily to be massacred
for the benefit of every person.
- God's plan was successful due to the
cooperation of the Jewish elite.

Because of that false accusation, the Jewish
nation needs to forgive Christians for two thousand
years of separation. It is the most profound issue
to resolve now because Jesus Christ is coming
back; as He proclaimed before ascension.

It will be a shame for everyone if the second coming of the Messiah happens while Jews are still waiting for their FIRST ONE!
In my dream, I have seen Jesus covering the whole sky – this is one of His predicted signs.
And my Dreams Come True if this time, all Jews and Gentiles receive Jesus with their opened arms and hearts.

Jesus in Hebrew is Yeshua which means "God saves, restores, and delivers." Just ask God, in the name of Jesus, for the precious Blood to purchase you back from the possession of the enemy.
Repent for your sins and have Faith - There will be no "NO response" for your request.

God achieved His goal thanks to Jew's disbelief in their Messiah!
Thus their doubt must have established Jews rescue from all sins, and no Jew needs to believe in Jesus to meet Him at the gate to Eternity!
However, it would clear up the fog of that ancient history if Jews recognised their blindness which was imposed by God to assure the compliance of His idea of salvation.

God's justice has been adjusted – our God is Genius!

And I will not reveal the mystery very soon - oh, maybe in the next book.
You will instantly understand what it means to be blinded!

In a nutshell, everything is OK – the rest of humankind also will be saved if everyone decides to believe that Jesus is the Saviour.
I totally agree with God - in my judgement of our Master.

To Be or Not to Be; – you can also find God in between! Is He not EVERYWHERE?

Christ Mission

Though my explanation may sound like a paradox, it is not. No Jew has to believe in Jesus, yet they are all saved in the first place.

For that mission of the Christ to save all God's children - to exchange Life for Life, Jesus had to be born into the Earth and exist publically in this earthly life as the evidence that He was one of the human population. In most ordinary circumstances, Jesus was able to grow and carry God's Blood and then voluntarily could undergo and withstand that unbelievable sacrifice.

Before the arrest, Jesus with disciples went out to a garden, over to Brook Kidron, and there Jesus confronted and took on Himself the sins of the world for which He volunteered to die. His sweat was trickling like blood.

Just before leaving to the garden, Jesus had said ***"Father, the hour has come. Glorify Your Son, that your Son may also glorify You. ...***

... And now, o Father "glorify Me together with Yourself, with the glory I had with You before the world was..." *(John 17:1-5)*

Who helped to release that glory for your benefit? Who crowned the fulfilment of the rescue project for the world, including you and me?
-   The Jews.

Kindly remember; it's Me who passed this knowledge to you. Thus, share with me the benefits of the cosmic Law of Gratitude, whenever you silently bless a passer-by, Jew.

Father God always can appear out of the blue as a man to you – He had already spent some time with Abram. However, to save the whole humankind from all sins – God had to observe all His Divine Laws very strictly.

Thus, by the intervention of the Holy Spirit, God's Life Essence was planted into a womb of a virgin female who agreed to be a "foster mother" to give birth to an ordinary boy who would be later recognised as the Son of God. At the time, Mary did not know that the boy was born to die for us all. Jesus, as Son of God, received full care from both Foster Parents because Archangel Gabriel asked Joseph to marry the virgin, Mary.

God was born in the flesh on the Earth; this lowered the frequency of His energy, and in that earthly existence, God is called "Jesus Christ or God's Son".

Jesus had acted diplomatically intending to become the Lamb of God for incoming Passover; to shed God's BLOOD for redemptions of sins for the whole world, with INTENTION to set up a New Covenant with all humankind. No more old rituals and ceremonies for purification of sins.

The last words on the cross: "Father, why did you abandon me" is not a complain.

It is a Testimony left by a man called Jesus Christ informing in the very end that He did not receive any help during the process of volunteered scarification; no supportive eyes of the Father, no singing angels!

There was hatred and screams of condemnation, strip and mock and extreme pain in most humiliating real moments; HORROR!

IT IS FINISHED – were the very last words. Father, in your hands...

    Whatever Jesus said or did – and is recorded in the Bible – every iota can be for your personal benefit; to take, to claim, to follow - in the name of Jesus Christ. In the next books, I will explain how. By the mean of Faith, with Jesus in a vision, everyone believer can perform the same miracles as the Son of God. You are the One, aren't you? Adjust yourself fully in this role – there are already thousands of people performing miracles more astonishing than Jesus did!

    After His death and Resurrection, Jesus returned to His right seat in the Throne of Trinity. Many visitors to Heaven could see that Jesus can merge with the Father God in the centre of the Throne and would appear back from that centre as Jesus.
Our Saviour in Heaven is equal, the same powerful God as the Father God in Spirit.
(John 10:30-31) When Jesus said, "My Father and I are One" - then the mob took up stones again to stone Him.

On sidroth.org/television, you can see and hear Interviews by Sid Roth with those who came back after death, and those who visited God in Heaven by invitation.

Back to EARTH - Open University

For what reason God cultivated the Tree of Good and Bad in the garden of Eden? Why did He allow the snake to live among them?

As likely as not, the destiny encoded in the forbidden fruit served as a kind of biological-spiritual disc designed for humans to step down from paradise into already developed Nature, ready to embrace and host them.
The Earth was a perfect area to become an artist in creativity and curve personal and corporative "WHO YOU ARE" on the way of transforming the density of the matter again into the Light.
Are you a member of a gym? Do you compete in sports events, do you take part in the Olympics? Do you know the thrill of engaging into a hard task, drop some sweat and win, while others are singing your name towards the heights designed for legends?

God knows perfectly well that human nature is vulnerable to sin, that it is easier or sweeter to slither into the side of Bad than to follow the path of righteousness. The resignation from the pleasure of forbidden delight may cause suffering - thus, constant raising from every fall fuels your engine of personal growth on the ladder up to God.

By choosing Good, you "suffer" your way in the process of transformation towards blossoming – the peak of the beauty in Nature.

Snake told lies that eating the fruit would give knowledge – or it forgot to mention that such wisdom is available only one the way of personal experience. Adam and Eve had to study the Good and Bad "at the open university of Life."

At first, there was not much capacity for action in the area called Bad– God had set boundaries guarded by pain or hurt, many emotions of fear or hate, envy, jealousy... you know all of them. Every single of them can cause a feeling of discomfort, misery, distress.

You will automatically know in your heart which is Good and which is Bad. Additionally, your Bad action is usually harmful to you and another person. Other people and the voice from your heart will advise you that it is easier and wiser to step back into the field of Good conduct.

Evil spirit activates

The vast problem occurred when evil spirits started to whisper to people and unceasingly try to lead them in the dark. Everyone could get lost, entangled in a weed of intrigues. There would be more reasons to gear all your negative emotions; you can start hating yourself but even more the other person or situation. And then, nothing good has a chance to germinate in your mind, nothing pleasant can pierce the sticky thickness of your energy field and please you from inside.

Have you ever considered that no animals, insects behave crazily; their activities are aligned to their true nature and serve the purpose of their existence fully? They lead utterly devotional life; watch any black fly. Will it return to lay eggs on your meat prepared to sacrifice its life? No sick bee would stay in bed - would fly closer to the hive to collect sweet treasure.

Will my answer satisfy your curiosity that they have no evil spirits to stir their common sense, to put on fire expectations and anger of disappointment. These living creatures make no plans for hurting or killing just for access to additional recourses after winning.
Evil spirits are not interested in these other living creatures; they are focused only on human beings!

WHY!
Why they tempt you into action solely on the Bad
field while beating new records in cruelty while
expanding negative boundaries, painful and tragic
not only for your sister and brothers but also for
your inner Self?
Who can explain such unwise behaviour of
intelligent people?

The answer is simple – it proves an incredible
intelligence and the power of evil. The enemy
knows very well that God will never condemn a
sinful man; personally and speedily, with the help
of the enemy, you alone will separate yourself
from God, you will lose your courage to get closer
to your Father. I chose to become an atheist just
because of a few very silly childish sins which
were mortal in my consciousness due to
unprofessional Religion teachers, cruel unwise
preachers in the church.

Deeper into the Darker

"Abide in me and I in you." John 15:4.
If you are not rooted in the biblical vine, if you are
not protected by Jesus' Blood, you have no
chance to win with any devil force!
Whenever one evil spirit cannot cope, it will bring a

few others to brainwash you. The most skilful liars get occupied with more significant people; the riches, the rulers, the church authorities. If you do not pray for them, it is almost impossible for these notable individuals to act in an honourable way. The noblest ones have many secrets in their sleeves; so many cases of hidden abuse conducted by the elite have been revealed in recent years.

If the masses of the population keep unfriendly thoughts or hatred towards their elite – these people in responsible positions become so much more vulnerable to evil.
It happens because of you; you -you-you, who is still reading this book written only to you.

No, sorry for the offence! I am talking about the others whom you know; they increase dark energy around people on the pedestal of power by unfriendly or nasty thoughts. You know it, because whenever everyone is mocking them - you do not try to defend, you are silent!
And at that moment exactly devil expands to them enticing opportunities.

Satan tried to allure a man called Jesus - "Jump from the temple of Jerusalem, God will send angels to catch you... as it is written in Scriptures."

What a perspective, what a spectacle - probably with the music of the spheres? No more wondering, no more forcible teaching to convince the crowds - Jesus' significance in the world would spread much quicker by word of mouth. "I will see to it to die later" - Jesus could have tried to persuade himself... As I expect, at the time of temptations, Jesus had to cope with Satan by himself - engaging only his human nature.

What would God do? Allow Jesus to die - or would send His angels to catch Him - but what consequences?

"god is following me, god acts as I wish, I was longing for this time for so long" Satan's victory would thunder across the Universe... god has passed on ME the rains!

We would live in another world now, rained by Satan personally!

Jesus did not allow to develop any base for discussion, did not get involved in empty yet cute arguments with the evil spirit.
No human intellect can win with the devil; Jesus did not rely on his brain - He used the Word from Scriptures to get rid of evil spirits.
What about your preferences? Confine to me secretly; you want it darker, heavier... or Lighter, brighter... what is your style of life? How do you

cope with evil influence, tell me?
Watch for them around yourself; identify if there is any and omit - do not forget to bless them quietly.

Let's return to the elite of our society after that short digression. With your hands, you can throw at them eggs, more damage you will deliver with harmful thoughts. Firstly, it is not possible to miss - your negative feelings and words will precisely deliver any gluey disgust which sticks to your victim like phlegm in repulsive colours. Psychic people can see it.

If you are a walking angel going around feeding homeless and stray animals...
If you are emptying your wardrobes for the poor or even if you don't believe in my words...

It should not cost you to flash your being with the colours of the rainbow - while engaging your thoughts only. Then surround yourself with a golden bubble. Do it three times daily as a part of your hygiene; besides, it doesn't take time at all. Or, even better, purify yourself with Divine Blood, and draw a protective circle around yourself.

"At first, lead the one worthy of attention astray. The idols would bring you more followers if you bewitched them by the art of tattoo..." Imagine how dad Satan gives advice newly trained demons

while patting their back - *"Off you go to people, my smart!"*

Be vigilant not to create a paradise for the enemy. A great triumph in demons dwellings to seduce the cream of society – through them, actively and passively, they will destroy the life and mood of the millions.
What a delight for Satan and his devoted team to win a noble soul forever, to increase the collection of earthly gems known and famous by their names.
The devils do not care about you that much, you the average member of the population. You do present the value as an image of God, but you will get freshly trained, newly acquired seducers – to assist you into the path of evil, the path of separation from Divine.

Be glad - you do present the highest value for your Father God - on the same highest level as all the others! As a soul, you had the same highest potential, but God could not put all the best colours in the centre of a picture.

I drooled that much to enforce in you the most predominated duty to love your riches, love your rulers! Anonymously, you will inspire them to work harder for society; send them love just for your own sake - pray for them. They chose their position on the top of the ladder to serve you; help them to survive during this most ungrateful task.

You need to remember that Lucifer was one of the most excellent Angels. He possessed much of Divine knowledge about cosmic network of legislation which governs our Universe. EVERYTHING in God's world is embraced and relies on the most strict Divine Law. "Until heaven and earth pass away, not a single iota or line will change in the law..." [Matt. 5:18].

Lucifer felt equal to God thus invented that all heaven should worship him on the throne, and managed to seduce one-third of angels for his support.
When God cast them all out of Heaven into the darkness, what Lucifer did with his companions?

He developed the entire region called Hell. Powered by his hatred towards God, the enemy is determined to catch the whole population of these tiny images of the Almighty; like you and me.
An effortless task for them with the individuals who became confused and vulnerable in his or her state of detachment - the people proud to cope without need to be rooted in God.
"Abide in Me and ask Me to help you" – is the request from God.

Otherwise, Satan will continue to succeed in collecting God's beloved creation and torture them. By doing so – the enemy feels the pleasure of torturing God – while repeating to you "there is no God."

Out of RESPONSIBILITY

Feel free to reject famous quotes that God "loves you so much" that He volunteered to be massacred for you!

Change your thinking; let's assume that God did what He did out of RESPONSIBILITY for His world and for the victimised people by Satan!
You would do the same if you were in His place, however wicked you are at the moment!

Thus, do not reject His Gift of Redemption. It is your right and opportunity to be saved from unspoken terror in the abyss of Hell. It is a cheque earned for you as the result of God's equally unspoken horror of sacrifice as a human!
Show your Responsibility for your life and your ETERNITY.

Be kind to yourself and helpful to God! Experience the delightful feelings after purification!

God has already suffered and paid for you anyway!

Jesus accomplished every iota of the plan. In the end, He uttered: It is finished! There is a newly revealed power in these three words, granted to people recently.

If you cannot wait for the next book, put your PROBLEM at the back of your head. Create the vision of Jesus dying, saying these words for you, "IT IS FINISHED"- repeat after Him with Faith. At the same time, see your problem dying for you, too.
Whatever Jesus accomplished, said – can be used personally by Faith for your benefit.

Have I already let you know that God is three times OMNI because He is entirely PRESENT, POTENT, and the third OMNI is better to understand as absolutely All-knowing, All-wise, and All-seeing?

Take advantage of every God's gift, benefit the most of it, implement in your life, apply in every trouble, and stop being a rebel! You are the son of incredibly ALMIGHTY GOD, unlimited in supplying whatever a human mind can believe. Claim it with Authority, Drag it through Faith, grab with mind or hands; be persistent but sometimes show a bit of patience.

How do you feel if your baby is coughing badly but refused your homemade syrup?
Earlier, she rejected the scarf you knitted, caring for the pattern so patiently.
My baby, how it feels when your mummy treaded on the bunch of wild little daisies you collected for her diligently?

By the way, put yourself in God's place - how it feels to see that more and more people neglect God's sacrifice, i.e. the horror of that massacre, that people deny God's Mercy? Instead, they blame God for the consequences of breaking the law and God commandments!
They do not have a second to spend with God, to ask for advice, for help?
Ponder on this from every aspect of mind and heart, however good or evil you are!

If you do not like soft arguments, let's try a harder way, tell me:
Do you love money – say it louder, I can't hear you!

Ok, I will continue with my drilling anyway.
Whatever is your mindset currently, consider the price and value of the Blood figuratively as cash, as the most priceless currency!

Would you want it, could you have it?
God's Blood has the right to be priceless. Do not waste that substance because chasing for your treasures was probably sinful – thus you need devilishly badly the rescue by the Power of that Blood, sorry, Cash.
And guess what!
God's greatest desire is to share the precious Currency with you abundantly. Take it as much as you need, sprinkle the Blood like golden confetti over yourself, become Jesus' bride. It cannot be simpler. A bride has no gender in the Spirit world.

Divine Love for you

– Be Holy because I AM HOLY, Be Good because I AM GOOD.

– Be Like Me, because you are Me – even by the Image.

Never mind the reasons, God's Love is unconditional. You are always perfect enough for Him.
Just as daily hygiene, use His precious Blood to wash away your sins.

   That God loves you; there is nothing unusual in it because Love is His nature. God cannot be different. As I wrote earlier – even a big black fly would sacrifice its life to nest its eggs in best environment - on a piece of raw meat.

Thus God cannot be less than ... Oh, oh my God, Man!
God can't live without you because you are His creation, the cell of His body. He feels your pain as His own – you are part of Him with "false" attribute of detachment.

   Your purpose of such detached existence is to create and transform your environment while adapting it to your needs; you become your own personal creative God is the beauty of such role in your life.
Many young couples leave their rich homes and start from scratch, many children of famous parents proceed the enrolment to universities under a false name. Many people do not want any help with finding a good job – they want to achieve everything themselves!

Be yourself, as You Are – don't cry for the world to please or accept you!

Only God is Understanding and Love – thus only God can truly love you,

Without your permission, without your knowledge, without gratitude.

Let's end this chapter; let Him Be! Do not exalt him, do not praise,

He is as He is – and cannot be different!

He is already in His perfect state - lack of love from you is His only pain.

To ensure the good fruit of your performance - God only hopes to be recognised as a lodger in your heart.
That artificial separateness was meant to provide you with a great deal of happiness and pleasure - the desire of God's heart to make you feel amazing with your choice and possibility of greatness.

Let's read how converted Apostle Paul described Love – the one who had a pleasure to torture the first believers in Jesus. It is a copy from the Bible, Corinthians 13 New International Version (NIV)

" If I speak in the tongues[a] of men or of angels, but do not have love, I am only a resounding gong or a clanging cymbal.

2 If I have the gift of prophecy and can fathom all mysteries and all knowledge, and if I have a faith that can move mountains, but do not have love, I am nothing.

3 If I give all I possess to the poor and give over my body to hardship that I may boast,[b] but do not have love, I gain nothing.

4 Love is patient, love is kind. It does not envy, it does not boast, it is not proud.

5 It does not dishonor others, it is not self-seeking, it is not easily angered, it keeps no record of wrongs.

6 Love does not delight in evil but rejoices with the truth.

7 It always protects, always trusts, always hopes, always perseveres.

8 Love never fails. But where there are prophecies, they will cease; where there are tongues, they will be stilled; where there is knowledge, it will pass away.

9 For we know in part and we prophesy in part,

10 but when completeness comes, what is in part disappears.

11 When I was a child, I talked like a child, I thought like a child, I reasoned like a child. When I became a man, I put the ways of childhood behind me.

12 For now we see only a reflection as in a mirror; then we shall see face to face. Now I know in part; then I shall know fully, even as I am fully known.

13 And now these three remain: Faith, hope and love. But the greatest of these is love."

Do not sound as simple as a clanging cymbal; may your ideas attune with the finest instruments.

Only ETERNITY Counts

All the time, the enemy knows your state of consciousness, your inner turbulence. If you are on your own, it is easy to lead you into a cluster of wicked thoughts and plans. The enemy knows how to open your case in your Book of Life to accuse you in respect of the breach of Divine Law.

You have all your cases lost if you don't repent and ask Jesus to forgive you – to clear up everything by the Power of His Blood – to erase every single sin. Make this ritual as the ongoing and endless process – but even in the last second of your life, only one-word BLOOD while thinking about Jesus can unite you with God and clear up all that sinful ballast. Like on Google, in one second, you close down one file or as many as you need.

If you prefer to stay apart from God, when your life ends, when your deeds are on the scales, it is easy to see to whom you belong. The scales will bow to the left or right, will show who fuelled you and gave ideas for your action along your path of life.

When the scales tilt to the left, you are lost to God; you belong to Satan according to your own will and life choices. You chose evil ways to become smarter than others, to become more famous... to achieve more in a shorter time, to go higher with smaller effort.

If you had prayed to God for help instead, you would have achieved even more – but as with everything, it is your Will to decide:

HOW DO YOU WANT TO SPEND ETERNITY?
WHERE DO YOU WANT TO SPEND ETERNITY?
But it is not too late to choose as you can still decide.
You can decide now because you are still alive.

Is it not the same reality at your home? You may prefer to live on the means of a bank. Sooner or later, the people in black uniforms will come to claim your possession. If no money to pay off, they will seize your wealth with you on the top - unless your parent pays for you.

It is the right moment to remind you that Jesus allowed himself to be massacred for your rescue and restoration.

Jesus' BLOOD to Rescue – Restore – Deliver.
Blood is Life. Life for Life is an equal exchange.

God's BLOOD for God's LIFE is enough as the payment for All of God's creation.
God is All That exists; Jesus gave you enough Cash for your Redemption.

The loss of blood on the cross was Father God's Blood which circulated in Jesus' veins.
The loss of that Divine Blood ended His Son's life.
The priceless Blood becomes like cash in the bank, available for taking for free by everyone to wash away their errors of misconduct, ask for it - use it in Jesus name.
Do not let me think that Jesus was massacred in vain.

Virgin Mary was chosen to grow the baby and deliver God's Life into the earthly ground.

It is easier to understand nowadays that Virgin Mary has agreed to become a vessel – as a foster mother. Archangel Gabriel could not use such expression out of people's vocabulary.
The Science discovery states that the mother's blood cannot mix with the blood of her child; separate DNA and metabolism governs the grow every foetus. After birth, the baby belongs to genuine parents, not to a foster mother.
 Holy Spirit implanted the spark of God's Life in Mary's womb; the baby's blood was fully Divine in origin - Jesus was the Son of God.

   The power of Divine Blood is your way and the gate to Heaven – it takes friction of a second to use it in the name of Jesus, even in your last moment.
Even better to keep clean and pure as a diamond by performing wine and bread symbol daily.

 You can also ask God to transform your food symbolically into Jesus' Body and Blood, and always stay in communion with the Divine. Just ask God every day for such a transformation. Take communion in a church if you are Catholic.

   However, remember that Jesus is not attached to any religion. God sent Him to the Jewish nation; all other people, i.e. Gentiles, need only to believe that He is the Saviour.

Greatest Sinners or Gems? Your ABCDEFG.

I will not call you by name. I hope you will guess that these words written more **A**ffectionately than **B**ravely to **C**osset you into the **D**iet of transformed bread and wine – are **D**irected **E**specially **F**or the most **F**inest **G**roup.

It is the greatest sinners obligation to rescue God from suffering that he had not suffered for you in vain.

I wrote the same earlier as a general request having this group in my mind.
Thus again: receive now God's Grace and your chance to be saved from a future residence in Hell. Be responsible for your Being and ecstasy of all the other souls in Heaven – they could not be happy without you! And your Father God would cry:

"You are my Soul – I Am your true essence.

I allowed myself to be crucified,

To beautify you with innocence!

Ask me, let me help you in every moment.

Use Me, unite with Me with Bread and Wine,

Such daily Hygiene will make you shine."

Look around, are you alone? Can you roar now; Jesus be my Lord! Sparkle me with your Blood.

Empty your memory, God doesn't want to penetrate what is covered by Blood, once forgiven it becomes automatically forgotten, vanishes from the Akashi records in the Book of your life.
 I'll let you know how God "punished me" for repetitive asking forgiveness of the same case of sin.
Place your expectation of forgiveness in Faith; this is the link which keeps you attached to God. Faith is enough for you to open the gates to chambers of His heart.

Do not torture God by trading your way to Hell; He can neither live nor Be without you - He cannot withstand your pain. God doesn't decide to Be Good – He IS - He is GOOD & LOVE in His essence and cannot be different.
God invented the most ingenious plan, ALLOWED HIMSELF to BE MASSACRED to pay for your burden and get you back. But even so, the enemy dances with human images of God singing the satanic song that God doesn't exist! What a nuisance!

Do you want me to repeat slowly? I will.

What a dreadful nuisance! While twirling around, everyone can see the Nature in its glory at every stage of effortless growth – being alive without pause. All that is also God visible all around, leading the process called Life in Abundance - in front of everyone's eyes.

God is Life – Life is God in the mood of Being and growing. God grows your body without asking for your permission – without your attention, awareness and supervision. In this process, you do abide in God – you have only a tiny false aspect of detachment where personality argues with Divine influence – do allow yourself to lose only this one battle.

Jesus suffered the most for the biggest sinners. They were worthy of sacrifice and torture; they won the title to be called the most precious gems in Jesus' collection. They deserved a more significant amount of Jesus Blood – He suffered longer because of them. Why? Because they were so valuable to Jesus. The mansion built for them in Heaven cannot be empty, no soul passing by such closed-door could enjoy eternal life and love.

What I say - everything is written in the Bible. Every Word there is alive; every Word keeps its power. Bible is a living computer to be decoded with a crystal clear software of interpretation which can be downloaded to any person if such is God's will. Even disciples seldom understood what Jesus said and what He meant. Sometimes you must seek more clarification, and sometimes, you do not focus properly, do not pay close attention.

When we are all together sitting on God laps, maybe, one day, we will tempt Lucifer to come back as well. When we break up with the song; *Come back the Morning Star, come back,* we will see what happens.

YOU – the Power

Jesus, as God in the flesh has created you to be the grand person able to handle the enormous power of the Universe. That's right - YOU - the misery hardly accepted in your mirror, a dot on the earth, a particle of a speck of dust comparing to the vastness of space!

How do you utilise your potential? It depends on the texture of your thoughts. If something goes wrong, stand your ground (close your windows and doors) and with authority shout "Nooooo..." to any negativity. By the Divine Law, the enemy cannot act against your will.

Just be aware that all possible entities watch you all the time. Thus, if you take a pill against coming illness, it reads as you have AGREED, you surrendered to demons. You must admit and agree that you have something already IN to fight it with medicine.
If you say NO with authority, no virus has the right to enter your body and feel at home; it has do die. Better claim: "I AM a child of most greatest GOD, the King of Kings – there is no illness in me, in God's home." And you can swallow any tablet to purify, to beautify your interior; be careful to name your intention correctly.

Did you not know that God expects to participate in your every business? He will rescue you from every disaster if you call for help – but agree to listen for the answer. And always be aware that having His powerful Will, you can resist misfortunes to enter your reality.
 Do not agree to a problem by saying confidently with the highest authority, "In the name of God, NO, I do not agree!" Say it as if to the Universe – your partner for life but see Jesus in your vision, never that problem!
 Please never focus on the problem, do not feed it with your emotions and energy. If you keep the vision of Jesus, you are absorbing the solutions,

the threat and end of any problem. Hear Jesus saying: "It is finished."

And remember to crush every crisis in the bud.

Although I plan to write soon at least ten books, already in the next one I will explain how my expanded problems led me to receive a rebuke from God: "I ALLOWED MYSELF TO BE MASSACRED FOR YOU", and how I could have avoided my torment.

Every moment can be your wake-up call; you have the power and the title to stand on your feet and claim your rights, to transform adverse outcome and benefit from it. In so-called past errors, there is your stored energy to bounce you up.

I am granting you again my permission to put this book away on the top shelf; promises are made to be kept, are they not?

Yet, I would be happy to meet you in the next chapter, пока!

CHAPTER TWO

COME BACK MY SON, COME BACK...

You, my Beloved!
Stand up for yourself in the most crucial issues.
Your decision about WHERE and HOW could prove pivotal;
Definitely will be critical at the end of devilishly short life.
WHERE DO YOU WANT TO SPEND ETERNITY?
HOW DO YOU WANT TO SPEND ETERNITY?
Better choose now when you can still decide!
You'd better decide now while you are still alive;
Because the whole Heaven cares for your eternal joy!
The Heaven sings: Come Back my Son, Come Back!

I Allowed Myself to Be Massacred

To collect you – FOR ETERNITY – all on my lap.

My early days

"Return my son - come back - your Father is waiting".

I heard this song deep in my essence probably in the cradle; maybe we are all born with this call?

This bewailing song stirred every molecule of my being – no other emotion could stifle that lament - and continues to reverberate to this day. It could kill your Soul if Soul existed; I used to think.
No wonder that eventually, the tale of prodigal son emerged at the top of this book.

I was born very wise and started to read from the age of three. Before I could correctly convert individual letters into sounds and collect them into one word – my uncle Helbik was delighted by my reading of the Bible, whenever he was busy with woodwork.
Very often, my struggle with fluent pronouncing proved to be so difficult; but the uncle could tell me the word as if someone sent him out of the blue.
I accused him that he knew the Bible by heart only is provoking me to read to keep my hands also occupied. After years, I realised it was the naked truth because I tried to assist him with carpenter's very sharp tools.

Anyway, the whole reading experience must have sharpened my mind too, especially that very often we were leading heated arguments. I was fiercely defending Christianity; the uncle was forcing and enticing me to become Jehovah Witness.
At such an early age, I already knew that changing your religion could send you to hell!
Although I had remembered every word from local preachers, often I was short of arguments - it seemed impossible to compete with the uncle who kept the Bible in the tip of his fingers!

There were moments that my emotions would twirl, swirl, whirl, twist and spin. Sometimes, I could not cope with overloads of feelings.
I was asking my mother to stop the uncle, but she was looking up to her oldest brother.
Or was it the only place she could leave me during travelling? There were no caring services in the village.

I needed a kind of protection intensely. I was already four or five on one sunny day, and in the moment of despair, but also mesmerised but the beauty of surrounding fields, I raised my hands to unite with God.
By raising my hands, unconsciously, I changed my offering into a Decree, and I had the impression that something clicked. I also committed myself to

write books; I chose a title at the same moment.
Then my parents built a new house. The windows
from my bedroom overlooked the place of my
contact with God in the field.

After reaching my age counted in teens, the
clever Me preferred to plunge in the knowledge
that God doesn't exist. I adopted a convincing
philosophy that your Believe system is a
background for judgement. If there is no God, I
had calculated, then the concept of sin dissipates.
It should be enough to observe moral standards
and ethics without a petrifying fear that some of
my actions could offend The Almighty God.
I was a positive person, well-read, and did not
need anybody from outside to guide or instruct,
God forbid - reprimand.

Yet, I could feel that God tried to snipe every
vapour of my mind, that He was pinching every
muscle of my heart, that He worked how to crack
into my consciousness!
He wouldn't go away, wouldn't leave me alone and
at peace.
Thus, forcing myself to live in the awareness that
He doesn't exist - I had to fight daily battles as if
God were there with me, in me, everywhere
around, all the time!
I lived in a real hell, one would admit.

As a wise and educated teenager, I equated that inner turbulence to the role of the subconscious mind which governs the body from inside.

Subconscious also bothers that an offspring respects rules and habits prevailing in their environment; it takes care that one wouldn't cross the borders.

I compared subconscious to a gardener dog that makes sure that the apple does not fall too far from the apple tree – in the role of the fence would be an imminent punishment.

Yet the things were getting worse. Very often would invade me a torment by a short and very poetic poem which I loved very much but could never remember it by heart - until now!

I would rip up a concrete wall If I knew I would find behind it these words.

Thus, I had to mesmerise myself by repeating two sentences hoping to trigger the memory and recall more. That poem wrote Kazimierz Przerwa-Tetmajer, whom I describe, "do not try to comprehend this author with the brain, do not try to translate..."

In English, these sentences I kept repeating would sound like:

"As if hanging on a bright ribbon or as if suspended on the bright ribbon... Is based on their

power... In their Soul, able to cradle/ sway the universe..."
Just now, I became aware that the Title of the poem is "The Word".

Yet, I kept suppressing the author's repetitive message; –"**May powerful YOU acknowledge that you are only inserted into the atmosphere of the Earth for a while – while being attached to the heart of God through the invisible ribbon of love**."

And then, after many years, it happened that I migrated to another city and received a flat on the 4th floor. I opened the big windows of my Living room and the door to the balcony, and guess what I could see?

What a nasty joke! There was in direct eyesight the altar of the nearest church of Saint Barbary!

And could you predict the next attack?
The wailing music was calling for the return of a lost child!

Before every mass, the congregation was singing that my most dramatic song; Come back, my son, come back.
It sounded like a sob, but it echoed in me like a bomb.

Family ties

I was sensitive to music in general. Still, in adulthood, that melody was affecting my deepest feelings for parents waiting desperately for the return of a beloved child who doesn't write letters, doesn't arrive for family ceremonies.
In my early age, the media hardly existed, thus who got in touch, who visited us was an interest of the whole relative's circle or could become a public issue in small villages and towns.

Adults were very diligent in developing the duty of writing letters while bringing up children. Whenever I joined the elderly, they were always talking about ungrateful offspring who after a good education, would abandon and forget their home.

Such complains, planted in small children, were designed to increase liability for the old helpless parents – there were no social care services in my country and many others.
The adults intentionally put the responsibility and trust for their late age in children's fresh mind. However badly a rebel could behave after escaping from home, one custom was a must; everyone had to get in touch or arrive home for Christmas and Easter to have the meal together as a whole family. Otherwise, the family would search for their sheep as for a lost victim.

The waiting time for the arrival of a family member was a pain, really; every hour, we counted days. The name of such relative was pronounced a multitude of times daily - by every inmate.
The family ties were incredibly tight - there were no media, not even a radio to occupy the mind with something else.

Additionally, my father was working in a distant city. He was coming home every two weeks with suitcases full of goodness – waiting for father's return was anguish experienced in minutes from the moment he was getting ready to leave us.

Being brought up in such circumstances, I was sensitive and receptive to returning or arriving of any close person. Even if I were intensely engaged in any fascinating work, I often would drop what was in my hands and would rush to open the door; to meet behind a bewildered relative who was about to knock.

As a person responsive to music and impatient about the return of our loved ones – that most dramatic music of the church song was the best bait God could have invented to steal me back.

You see, the Almighty God, who is in direct touch with every particle of millions of galactic, has enough light to shine across and into all the nooks and crannies. God is flexible enough to bend and pick you up once He finds you. And He will try to keep you aside unless your equally Almighty Will - will create an impassable barrier for Him.

In my case, God obtained two goals at one shot. I was a tiny child when I broke a moral law while led astray by a song. And my mortal sin hidden in the background of my mind was the exact reason that I decided to convert into atheism. I tried to block any thought about the existence of God.

Oh My God

In my generation, many religious songs escalated the fear of God. The most popular glorified God-Mother Mary as the person who can defend people when angry God would flog you, chop you with a rod...

We were singing such songs every evening at home; almost impossible to translate into English the exact words.
Parents, siblings, friends, neighbours, strangers... without any more in-depth insight, everyone felt entitled to inflict the sting; "God will punish you."

I also was administering such threats to others, regardless of treating myself with the long period

of atheism.
Learning everything as early as from the cradle, I was unable to correctly interpret the sense of simple songs and poems while the text of lyrics strived to find the rhyme, aimed to stir the heart, did not care much how to convey the reality and the truth.

I kept taking in too early and too literally everything as it sounds and cemented the first impression for good.
Thus I perceived God as the watchful cruel judge and the most absorbing sponge of praising, worshipping.

To appease Him, I used to say morning and evening prayers with hands folded perfectly. I kept my skinny body straight while kneeling on my bony knees - and my feet separated sometimes. I was too weak to keep them aligned together. Such was my first mortal sin committed by disrespectful position while sharing the presence with God during prayer.

I was terrified of God, whether He existed or not. I had lived probably two years in the flat until I couldn't resist the sob of the song any more.
One Sunday, my resistance collapsed, and I joined in the middle of the church ceremony. I focused on the altar, which I could see from my Living room

and tried to get closer, but I was paralysed - by the sentence as if directed to me. I could have dropped dead hearing that God is Love and that He loves His creation!

That contradicted all I had ever heard from my parents – and the local church and religious lessons. My uncle enjoyed Armageddon most; God's wrath and punishment stayed on the tip of everyone's tongue, also mine.

God was on the guard of your righteousness; He will judge you for every thought, every misdeed on the scales of Justice as soon as you die. Then purgatory or hell. The devil is waiting for you and waving its tail - there is no escape.

And how easy it was to deserve the eternity in hell!

It was enough to omit the Mass on Sunday or eat meat on Friday. Unless you are lucky and whisper your sins to your priest during personal Confession, you are assuredly likely to end up in hell.
In our region, the famous biblical saying was valid alike for the rich and poor, "it is easier for a camel to go through the eye of a needle than to enter the kingdom of God."

There were no Bibles in households around; the Holy Book was out of print in the communist

country. Reading the one from other religions, Like my uncle's Jehovah version was also forbidden for me.
 The preaching in the church was the only source of my acquired knowledge and the breathtaking stories — the ones I liked best - until now, I can feel intensely in my essence. There were about a Samaritan woman and the prodigal son.

At those early days, I identified that beautiful church song "Come back, my son" with that biblical villain.
 As an adult, I learned the extended version of the story tale. If you don't object, I will share with you. I have to warn you that such family never existed. Jesus invented such allegory to describe the Heavenly Father as a character. His disciples, knowing Jesus as a man, became curious what to expect while returning to God, seeing Jesus on His right.

In recent years, I pondered deeper on this parable. I will add a little extension to disclose invisible threads and insights hidden in between; to arouse and satisfy your curiosity even without your request.
Nevertheless, are we not equal?
I also have to secure my right to charm myself with this delightful bit while reading my book, although I

write it only for you with the desire to please and appease and disarm as the primary goal.

Let's judge Jesus

So, according to our storyteller, God, the Father is precisely like Jesus; If you know me - you know the Father.
Thus, nobody to fear is my first conclusion.
 Jesus respected everyone; he never fought back. Jesus also taught something about the other cheek, but I am afraid to repeat knowing how difficult it is to tame rising emotions.

He saved a sinful woman by giving a quick verdict: - Who is without sin, may take a stone and be the first to throw it at her!
And then, immediately, as if oblivious what was going on, Jesus returned to drawing something on the ground probably with his finger – like a little boy.
How does it sound? Cool so far!
To be precise, the scribes and Pharisees brought to Jesus a woman caught in the very act of adultery. They intended to set a catch on Jesus as He was known for hanging out with sinners.

Imagine the scenery;
Without any doubt, there was clear and
overwhelming so-called naked physical exhibit; a
woman caught red-handed, standing most
probably half-naked among the raging mob.
I am sure you already detected little inconsistency;
if she sinned against the sixth Commandment of
God – was she there in that dramatic hour alone!
 Why did the religious righteous people not bring to
justice with that female the other part of the
sinning procedure – I mean the man!

The crowd was enraged; the scales of emotions
was out of balance, a shaking woman in the
middle! In such a clear case, Jesus ought to
honour the moral standards; He would have to do
the right thing; condemn the woman and back up
"the righteous" scribes and Pharisees!
We know that Jesus was fully aware of everything,
could read people's mind. How to explain that this
time He chose to ignore the situation and
continued with the writing on the ground?

Do you agree with me that during this drawing
in silence, Jesus was creating the psychological
background to hypnotise everyone with a sudden
bolt from the blue?
After long persistent requests for His opinion,
Jesus straightened up for a moment only to strike
them with wisdom brighter than any lightning: "He

that is without sin among you, let him first cast a stone at her."
Oh my God, everybody left!
Was everyone so modest?
Or, in the whole of Jerusalem, around the temple, there was no innocent icon?
Please contemplate on the vastness of evil while, simultaneously, I will continue to praise Jesus.

Let me only check your IQ first - Why and what was Jesus writing on the ground?
Put your answer on my Blog.

So, I was about to say that our Redeemer never raised His voice for any disobedience, never scolded any sinner, neither that adult adultery woman.
He never used bad words; God forbid - no cursing (once only he cursed a tree for not growing fruits, and it died soon).
Jesus was all the time open for a service, whoever asked, or sometimes without being asked.
While passing the funeral of a young man in Naim, Jesus raised him from the dead and returned the son to the lamenting mother, a poor widow.
He cast out demons from people often without request.
By the way, it indicates that acting at the spiritual level doesn't breach the person's will – definitely, we can pray for others.

I need to mention that our Saviour was not
afraid to crash social standards boldly if it could
win and restore other people's` respect or mindset.
As if an ordinary man, Jesus shared meals with
the margins of society sitting among them as their
equal.
He allowed a local female sinner to take care of
his feet – at the time when He arrived at a
prestigious home for dinner.
Nobody was repulsive to Him; even men affected
by leprosy could come close to receive help
through the touch of His hand.
Jesus was willing to help and wanted to help
everyone, whoever asked. He was very
responsive to people needs.
Although He famously said to Satan that not only
bread feeds the man - Jesus did provide plenty of
bread and fish to satiate a few thousand people in
the desert, who followed him to share his wisdom.
Jesus loved to share everything, all His knowledge
and skills – He was even willing to teach how to
walk on water if someone would be so childish.

Even disciples could not agree who indeed
Jesus was, but once He asked them "Who do you
say I am?"
And only Peter gave the correct answer, "You are
the Christ, the Son of the living God".
In truth, Jesus was looking for evidence, which

one of the disciples was most inspired. Then Jesus turns to Peter with such words; "Blessed are you, Simon son of Jonah because flesh and blood did not reveal this to you, but my Father in heaven..." (Matthew 16:17)
For some reason, Jesus was careful not to reveal the truth about Himself through His mouth. However, quite frequently, Jesus would unfold that He was not from this world!

I dare say that Jesus introduced Himself properly only to one woman. And her ears exclusively heard the divine secret of Jesus' world mission and purpose for coming as a Saviour. Women, in general, were not recognised in ancient society, but Jesus performed even more significant advance; He passed the mystery of His mission on the least worthy one.

That woman must have been an outcast of the society – as she came alone to Jacob's well at the heat of the day. She did not feel comfortable or was rejected to walk together with other women to fetch water for her household during the cooler part of the day.
The woman had to suffer incredible heat while walking thirsty and alone from her town to a distant field. During such a challenging way, a single

woman was likely to faint without any hope for
help.

Only once she met a stranger; a man, a Jew by
appearance, was sitting next to the well.
He was probably thirsty too; he did not have a pot
to reach the water – so deep in an ancient well on
that remote place, inheritance from Jacob.
Oh, I have galloped too far; this is my second
delight, the story about Samaritan woman.
I will leave the further piece of Biblical literature for
another chapter.

May this first glimpse into Samaritan woman only
enlarge the picture about personality and
character of that man who lived here as Jesus,
because He is coming back to us now, I saw His
enlarged figure as vast as the sky.

May these stories restore the credibility of His
teaching, the equality of all God's children through
Jesus while He intends to empower the weakest.
Just the very description of Jesus builds up the
picture of God the Father; They are alike and can
become ONE. Whether separate or Both in
unison, they can hide behind unimaginable
vibration of Energy and Light.

However, in the parable about the prodigal son,
Jesus left the most compelling personal evidence

for humankind what to expect when your time comes to face God.
The Soul may be confused at first glance - this narration exhibits the very nature of our Heavenly Father; how He responds to his children, especially the lost ones.
For their sake, God raised His Son on Earth to sacrifice His life.

After sharing with us the truth about Father God, soon, Jesus will fulfil God's project thanks to the cooperation with Jews.
Jesus keeps telling that He has to suffer and die - yet disciples are also like deaf and blind.

Thus, soon, while we are in the middle of the fable, the innocent Lamb will be lifted on the cross. Lots of Blood will gush out from first wounds on the head and His back, not much will be left when He climbs up to Calvary.
The bloodshed on the cross, the direct cause of death is the most precious and the most potent substance for purification of your sins.

Take it now, immediately, abundantly, as if most efficient washing liquid for your stored soot. Why scrub it in Purgatory if you can say even now at your computer desk, "Jesus be my Lord, I regret being bad, forgive me, cleanse me..."

*He is not an English teacher, the more confused
you become, the better. Then, Jesus will have to
look deeper at your secret rabble and select even
unknown to you grime.*

    This last-minute story about God the Father
Jesus had to invent deliberately as any
comparable example did not exist in reality of
those days.
You must agree with my conclusion that it was
God who introduced Himself to you through the
mouth of His Son Jesus - because Jesus never
acted on His own.

You have to evaluate that evidence as declaration
intended by God – "This is who I AM for you".
Why was I so scared of God? Why I spent almost
all my life in an inner terror?
I would say, this is two thousand years old portrait
of God you have to keep in your mind and eyes
while ramping around your affairs; yet strive to be
fair!

    Undoubtedly – the story implies that greetings
like prodigal son can expect every one of us
regardless of life achievements or conduct.
You have to trust my resolutions because Jesus
must have been aware of all the accompanying
incidents; He chose the background of the parable
consciously.

In consequence, read the story as I simplified for you below. Also, keep in mind that:
"Jesus could not have said more openly that His Heavenly Father and our God is an Entity without dignity - while searching around the horizon to find every lost person."
It is difficult to tell who is the most devoted Shepherd; God the Father or Jesus?

Should I put this question into the IQ quiz for you to discover?
No, this one would be too easy - Jesus and Father are both equally mad about you, beloved.

The story of the prodigal son.

Once upon the time, far away behind hundreds of miles, in a distant Israel lived a rich man, a father of two sons. He had an extensive estate, distinctive clothes and jewellery, vast fields growing many vineyards and animals. He had many servants, employed many labours... the sons also worked hard.

- Idyll, I hear you say!
- Yes, the patriarch was also in robust health.

And imagine now that one of them, the younger if it fires your wrath - boldly claimed his part of the estate so as he could live in his particular style! The law of inheritance, the customs, the habits, the respect for parents ... all that created the consciousness that everyone should drop dead hearing such meanness.
In straightforward meaning, such a demand speaks: "I wish you were dead, but instead of waiting for that moment, give me my part, and I am no longer here with you!"

- What!
- That's what you have heard!

In general - only after the natural death of a father could follow the execution of the inheritance. The young son demand was a severe insult - could invoke stoning him to death. The father had the legal and moral right to disinherit and disown such rascal.
At those days, in everyone's mindset, respect for the age was anchored very profoundly. But you can say the same about other factors: "Knock, and it will be open for you."
The son must have been consistent in tantalising his father because he gave him the full participation of his wealth; he fulfilled his son desire. The son left his home.

I do not know if the boy was tight-fisted or ... But the rumours about his extravagance were reaching the village where he was born.
I had better stop here and let your imagination draw you into the set of odds and chances in the circs possible even in those old days.
How long – how much – fancy to be a documentary film director.
If you can recognise a Jew somewhere on the track, stop him and try to set up a conversation about swine.

Sorry to put you in such an experience – but how could feel those people about their own man reaching the rock-bottom in a foreign country.
There was one solution to end up that shame – forget, remove him from memory, consider him lost and dead.
I know the prodigal son must have been abroad; pigs were not permitted to live in Israel; they would desecrate the holy land.

And now imagine that young man, now penniless, has desired to earn although a small change.
At last, he found a job - he started to care for animals.
Imagine something you are familiar with like a shepherd – only our hero was not so lucky, he became a swineherd!

Such a position is nowhere well-paid, no other additional benefits.

As Prodi is dead (easier to imagine him by name) and no longer recalled in his village, i.e. no longer exists in our side of the story - let's migrate to his area and stay in Prodi's shoes for a moment.

What can you see or feel?
Oh, no! The desire to share hog's food!
What's going on in his mind?
I do not wish to experience that.
Let's go back to the village.

We are just here back at the best moment. Look at that old fool running across the fields!
His robe is pulled up to enable speeding up!
He exposed his ugly old legs!
Very disgusting, undignified!
Could it be the owner of the estate, our patriarch?
What happened to him!
I can hear someone gossiping and giggling. "The FATHER is running, because he EXPECTED that the dot on the horizon might unfold into HIS SON COMING BACK!"
His eyes were scrutinising the horizon for all these years.

There was no much animation in the distance; the other person was strolling – the old one was running towards him!

You see, the elderly patriarch owner of a vast
vineyard should not have run at all in front of his
servants and labour. It's out of authority or self-
respect. I refuse to continue.

    When they met – it was a habit that the younger
would advance with greetings – but he did not
have any chance – the father embraced him and
proceeded with kissing.
I am sure the father did not receive such symbols
of gratitude from Prodi while granting him the
whole part of his inheritance.
Now, the prodigal son received all possible
amount of affection for squandering everything.

Prodi did not have a chance to blurt out his
repetitive monologue and then ask for a job.
And then the best clothes, sandals, a ring - and
the best dishes completed by music and dancing!
Hmmm! I am not sure if I am annoyed or baffled.
You better read this yourself in the Bible to check if
I tried to mislead you; if I crashed the walls beyond
naivety?

I can continue if you want but under another title,
because I have picked up that you are keenly
interested in the owner of that vast old vineyard.

The Father of prodigal son

So let's go back to dig into the parable because the whole picture holds still dark patches not fully answered.

Firstly, the owner of the estate could have stayed his ground, wait until the newcomer would approach him and then deal with his issue.

If indeed, it was the son who was returning, the father could have allowed Prodi to approach and apologise.

And then, Prodi could act out all rehearsals performed along the long way home.
 His life lesson would ingrain itself in his brain the hard way if he went through the prepared ritual of asking for forgiveness.

All the time he could watch and read the father's countenance, his desperate looks shooting around at people for advice.

Only then, after the happy end – I mean fathers forgiveness, local people approval, Prodi could request for a job and the right to stay under the roof like other servants. For a small remuneration package in a reward.

Would it not be a noble procedure to resolve the conflict in front of insiders who witnessed that father's hurt and humiliation in the first place?

You are my witness that everything here crossed the boundaries of rational expectation; though the two greatest Masters of our universe presents the story to humanity!
 Aren't you disappointed?

Who can guess why the older adult was running? Was it a desire to meet his son earlier? Or was it fear that young man might feel ashamed and change his mind and escape again? Or, the father wished to save his son from humility and wanted to grant forgiveness more rapidly?

Probably all these factors fused into one burning emotion to ensure that son is genuinely back – and, he could hold his son in his arms a bit sooner. And then! The best calf was ordained to land on the table, everything the best in abundance!
But now the time came to deal with the most crucial issue lurking from behind; the money!

What about the payment? Of course, all servants and workers participated in the Father's joy; somebody had to dance to obey the music.

No, I was not so foolish to suggest that he paid these participants for taking part in the entertainment, probably father paid only musicians.
I asked if anybody did pay or participated in the

cost of meals and dancing entertainment, they were hired to work in the vineyard, weren't they?

- Well, probably everyone was invited to the indicated position at the table.

You must be right. Nonetheless, in whatever manner workers spent the time; sitting or dancing, or eating and gossiping, or watching and enjoying themselves - all that must have been for free! What I was curious about was that payment for the job. The dole agreed for working in the fields! Were they paid for the task planned to finish in the vineyard on that day, or they postponed that activity to do freely on another day?

Sorry for the grill over arithmetic if you do not enjoy it.
Besides, if the story triggered your interest, I need to continue with drilling. Was the fable suggested by me or told by God - the Mastermind governing single molecules in every galactic on top of all black holes.

So tell me, can you see any justice or wisdom when the father gets so extravagant with expenses for the reception of his son who had squandered fathers blood, i.e. farm?

Let them enjoy the feast while you analyse for me please; "Were these servants paid for working in the fields at that time of celebrating the return of that shame? Did the Owner decrease workers daily rate? Or they did receive the agreed dole for the whole day? What is your guess?"

Shall I put the question in the IQ quiz? Certainly not, it would be dishonest of me and detrimental to your score in this complete maze.

Because my guess and the answer is: Certainly not! The workers did not put in their pockets the agreed sum of money - they put a bit more!
I am convinced that everyone received an extra bit in the form of a tip.

You agree with me that I had to be so conscientious about finances; the money issue was the starter theme of this fairy tale invented by Jesus.

My Masterpiece, please, do not judge the Master, because your Master is allowed to lose Himself in the Ministry of His Inner Affairs, whenever they are not in conflict with the cosmic legalistic.

FATHER GOD CAN SPOIL HIS RETIRING CHILDREN BEYOND HIS ABILITY AS IT IS UNLIMITED!

In my opinion, Jesus could have addressed disciples' curiosity shortly – for example, in such fashion! "Father God, like mad, will search and rescue and receive every one child!

And then He will restore everyone to his position and magnificence!"

 Such strict description would have closed the whole issue - I would not have had to write that much.

But Jesus likes long parables – what He will tell us upon His return now?

Most probably, at the very beginning, Jesus will let us know that the "Almighty OMNI-owner of billions of galactic is preparing a small Reception for his beloved little ones (you & me) on arriving back home with Me."

Wow, was that not too short?
Have I already told you that Jesus is coming back?
In my dream I saw Him as big as the sky!
Jesus kept saying that such would be a sign of His second coming!

Post factum of prodigal son.

I will add on my behave, that it was the Father God who has sent Himself to be massacred to redeem the naughty ones who kept breaking the law which governs everything - as above so below - also these clusters of visible galactic or hidden in black holes.

The institution of Satan diligently collected accusations for everyone's incidents into the file. If you sparkled yourself with Jesus' Blood, your file is covered, all facts are invisible under the Blood, all have vanished. Your file turns into a book – the cover shows up as a red varnish — no need for your cleansing by the fire element. Thus no ashes; even psychics couldn't read your history though no psychics reside in the Heaven.

In Heaven; Forgiven means utterly Forgotten.

And now Prodi also returned; he is safe, and secure, and delivered and restored to his dignity.

Let's contemplate longer to find the real cause of Prodi's escalation into his majesty, although he ashamed his father.
I hope you remember that son refused to work for their domestic possessions and demanded his part of the inheritance at a very young age.
Eventually, elderly Father must have been in great

anguish because he trod down the tradition and granted the rebel his wish.

The young man could not wait to leave his home. What happens next?

   In any era, BC or AD, money would not stick to your pocket; easy came – easy spent.
I do not like gossiping, nor bad words; you can learn more from rumours which reached the ears of all mates and friends.

It looks like in this world the lust can last and expect rewards and look for another cluster of luck with a good chance for a big fortune to back it up!

"... there is no pride, no bitterness, no shame what the others would say, no consideration to his own rules... there is obviously no justice in his attitude..."

- Who is churning these accusations?

"You can ponder and expand your opinion about that..."
Oh, I am lost myself what I am talking about, or who I am talking to? I am so highly confused!"

   Probably, jointly, I was in my shoes, and in sandals of that older hardworking son on his father's farm, who never had time for games, for any outings. He is trying the taste of their fresh wine with his friends now; they are saying such words...

I cannot use them because these words describing Prodi's lifestyle and about his father, I do not keep in my vocabulary; thus, let it be the end of this story.

   At last, we know for sure what to expect while coming back to live in Eternity.
 What kind of reception to expect from such Father God who shed His Blood to make Eternity readily available for everyone.
Put Jesus description on top of everything; "if you saw me, you saw the Father". It was Jesus who suffered to fulfil God's Idea of redemption.

Jesus in Hebrew is Yeshua which means "God saves, restores, and delivers."

In other words, God Jesus is the cause of your and Prodi's Splendour.
"Your" means whoever: the greatest sinners, the blocked atheists, the restricted accusers, the cruel rulers, the child abusers, the terrorists, the rapers, the human traffickers ... and me.

I am not sure now, but I used to have the ability of precise insights. Thus I will try to predict the rules in God's Estate. But let me remind your duty, you - a piece of the Master.

I shall try, no matter if it will soothe or infuriate you - a good son, and me - the holy one, if I say about our superiority of the reward?
It will work in such a manner - if you agree to read the next statements.
While residing at home, I mean in Heaven, every prodigal son will be more than happy that he has returned.
But the rest of us will exhaust in the ecstasy of happiness, for our prayers drove him on the right path that eventually he has managed to join us.

The bottom line is: our God designed our Spirit to intensify the thrill for any flaw transformed back into the Divine principles of symmetry.
Like our brain is established to exalt the effect created in accord with rules of the sacred geometry.

The second coming - Why Now?

And now, Jesus is coming back – I saw His large body stretched across the whole sky.

Why now?
Because we are all in distress: the young and old, the rich and poor.
The birds hardly sign.
The people stop greeting and smiling at each other.
The Earth still try to bewitch our eyes with a few colourful patches – but seldom one has time to admire, no time to leave home.

The soil is sick, depleted of minerals to pack into food, full of germs and unfriendly bacteria.
The crust of the Earth developed inflammatory spots like acne on facial appearance.
Can you hear Our Mother Earth's calls: detoxify - save me, restore, deliver! I surrender.
Oh, Jesus, come back! Detoxify our life or take us all to your space.

We wait for you with utmost impatience. We have infused the image of God as the father of prodigal son into our Faith, into our consciousness.

You have established the newest Covenant sealed by the shed of Divine Blood on the cross.

For that reason, You-God in Spirit allowed
Yourself to be massacred through Jesus – the
God in Flesh, performing as God's Son.

Now, we both know them both; God the Father
in Spirit and Jesus as God in the flesh; do not be
afraid to die and soar up to spend Eternity with
them.

The bottom line: They cannot live without me;
They cannot feel whole without you.

Sparkle the Blood in your imagination over you
and home and your loved ones, and you will be
united with God, free from invasion of devils, try
only to control your thoughts.

While staying in that unison, like a branch in a vine
– you will not be able to be torn apart; you will
build up instead of destroying.
Even if you trip over and fall – the request for
Blood will glue you again, and old staff will vanish
as if under a red varnish.

Do not be silly, would three times OMNI God
rummage in your old filth? Regret once only while
asking for forgiveness; once forgiven - forgotten
forever.

Stop Regretting

Let me tell you my story experienced as a grown-up girl. I visited relatives and noticed that their cow had scars around horns where the rope was attached to. I decided to take care of it, but I kept forgetting and then left the farm.

That grief started to haunt me in my adult life.

Very frequently, I felt very suppressed; I could not stop regretting. I kept sending love to all cows as fulfilment for my neglect.

Eventually, I started to torment God for help. I do not remember the first solutions as they did not change my feelings. The old memory stayed fresh, and my sorrow wouldn't end.

Finally, I asked for a meaningful, convincing dream which would visibly destroy my guilt.

On the first night, I received such a dream: I was standing close to the cow, and she embraced me with her neck, and after a while, gave me a tight hug.

At that moment, I could feel a vast multi-dimensional love flowing from the cow into my body. Besides, I was aware of a little discomfort; these animals do not have very flexible necks. To tighten a slim person in an embrace required a kind of energy and effort and was stressful for the cow.

Anyway, it was the cow's will to put a strain on herself, and that felt good altogether. I lived at peace but not very long - I started to look for reassurance.

What if my subconscious mind projected the dream?

After a little while, I sent another request to God.

The next vision was about the cow and me standing in a friendly mood opposite each other. The cow suddenly licked me on the right cheek and then kissed; I felt lots of drool dribbling down my cheek.

I woke up and jumped – "*Next time the cow will kiss you on your mouth, remember*" – such a thought was awaiting to shoot at me without warning!

Cows do produce a lot of salivae to lubricate their specific digestive pattern - all the time busy chewing the food.

God gives me natty dreams in the state of a masterpiece – there is often sweet punishment which adds to the cup of joy.

God knows that my saliva is unpleasant for me, how I resisted vomiting whenever my mother or sister put their spoon in my soup.

Thus treat my advice as received from authority with a lot of experience. In God's world, FORGIVEN equals FORGOTTEN for ETERNITY!

Have I convinced you? Or shall we process these big QUESTIONS again, HOW & WHERE?

Have you ever experienced the delight of purification?

Or let's check how you operate within the field of Faith.

Are you aware of, or you are already a practical user of constant Divine help?

Let's try this survey - with your little human brain; please answer these questions:

Can you anticipate the water to feel hard on you?

Would you ignite the fire to cool you?

Would you expect the air to resist your breath?

Has any liquid ever refused to make you wet?

Do you make plans for tomorrow before going to bed?

Let's check for the result! I am impatient about the overall score!

Hmmm, they say the survey is too short!

I might work out the expanded version, but later, this chapter has already oversized my goal.

Yet from your answers, I presume that you are an ordinary guy with a regular capacity for Faith.

Wow, nothing wrong with you. See you in Heaven!

When? You neither know the day nor the moment.

Before we part, as you may not be coming back, I would like to encourage you to read the Bible.

At first, choose only the most charming fables.

By reading the Holy Book with passion and love, you enhance the capacity of understanding, the unlimited power of memory, the power of vision, prediction, intuition... and in general, you grow into the Unity with God.

You will obtain a state of conversation with God without realising it – you will assume that you are thinking your own thoughts unless He will choose to speak to you loudly.

Only then will you know!

I am so impatient to tell you the story about my intimacy with God.

But I have to finish this chapter; again, it seems to be much too long.

CHAPTER THREE

BE LIKE ME

I AM HOLY - Be Holy

I AM GOOD - Be Good

I Allowed Myself to Be Massacred

To wash out your sins,

So as You can shine

Like a diamond in the sky

After such daily hygiene.

GREETINGS

"I called you in, Jeremiah 1:5 before you were in your mother's womb. I sanctified you before you were born. I wrote my plans for you in your book."

What a marvel! There must be a good reason that you are with us. Most probably we lack that specific radiance only you can shine.
You are a walking flower carefully planted on the earth; not at random place, not somewhere by accident. Undoubtedly, your particular role and the station were selected personally by the Divine Architect.
The Creator's desire for achievement through you is in His first finger - we are here to keep an eye that you make the exact imprint.

At your birth, God blew the Spirit of life in your nostrils - you took a glance in the beauty of your design because you screamed.
What a magical spell to her! You will recognise her voice in every corner of space from the moment she called you by name!
The mantra of every vowel and syllable, like an incantation, gurgled into Universe.
Simultaneously, as your mother spelt your name– you were registered in that instance.
The Universe certified your arriving into the very

centre of your existence. – the place of your birth.
Your fairy tale opened up on the first page.
Insert his picture – with suspended breath,
everyone whispered.
What another witchery image of God, everyone
exclaimed!
Soft incantation murmured your name across the
sky and waved you goodbye; from that moment
you are rooted on earth among us.

We heard your first cry, the rainbow of our
colours bowed to you; "You are Welcome."
With YOU - a new hue, we are here to melt and
stir and merge and blend any substance so that
they combine into new stuff or a matter.
What matters is, that we, collectively as a mass of
people, will deliver together a holistic benefit of
action that is greater than the sum of its
participants — a synergistic benefit, as in
Ayurveda effect. YOU will boost the phenomenon
of our cooperative achievement through your
devoted passion.

The whole plan for yours and our life may be
secret, but you will reveal it when resolving step by
step every daily commitment. Your heart desire
will pull you through, and farther, and higher -
towards your greatness!
What an endless pleasure if with full diligence, you

will tackle your current task and later you will realise that it was a part of a giant global design.

Whenever you gaze back – the multitude of processed stuff can look like a mountain. It would have been too overwhelming to begin something so colossal at the start; it could hold you back. It is the reason that you cannot see your mission because you are so modest. Only when you get involved in the action by surprise, and you love it - do not keep your horses in a stable – always give away your very best.
And then everyone will gossip; the Creator excelled again what and how to achieve through him -hear here "your name" - how to make the most of the best while using "Peter's" mind and hands.

In every remote place any minute task, every dot on a picture however dark – anything is an equally vital part of the enormously gigantic design; everything is entangled and relying on one another. The darkest blot on a face in the picture may become the most intriguing and magnetic spot. And you can accomplish your purpose by responding to every task of your daily life while following your heart impulse.

In other words, love every part and aspect of your job, look for an employer whose products and services will build up instead of destroying. But watch for hints within your family first, then at school, the society in your town and your country - they hold the key to your success.

Your energy field keeps all your records you need to help find co-partners for every success - whatever you need for life, look for the first supply and full polish up in your close circles. You will attract the teacher at the right time. Look around; it can be any small child. Go for the first impression; the entire world worked it out for you - God created the universe to serve you.

Now, I can't wait to share with you my unforgettable dream. It must have happened decades of years ago but is so suitable to support my freshly expressed ideas about individual passion leading to a cooperative miracle.

There was no particular reason, circumstances to have such a dream; it happened as if by itself and will stay in my memory forever.
In the village where I was born, there lives a very hardworking family named Kamas. They are fully committed to every aspect of the farm and job, whether they are doing it for themselves or others. There were many children born into this family; mostly boys.
From their spacious shed of numerous pigs and

cows, a bad smell was lingering around. The building was very close to the road; it was a sickening experience for me to walk by on my way to primary school.

In my dream, I was watching these small boys as adults. The shed was already pulled down, and boys intended to make a tiled floor within the existing foundation.
They did not have any design, any pictures, no training.
How did they start?
I watched five teenagers entering the area within the foundation. They did not discuss. In five random parts of the floor surface, next to their feet, five lay boys started to set up small tiles without any preparation. They did not hurry up; neither they watch one another, nor scrutinised their completed part of the whole.

There was no music of the spheres; in a pleasant silence and feel-good vibes, everyone adjusted small tiles as if in a trance.
One thing was striking - every one of them was entirely concentrated on his performance; hands, eyes and mind were unified into the action of the moment.
In a short time, the young men finished the floor.

Even in the dream, I was astonished by such an outstanding piece of art. The intricacy of the design, the sophistication of the pattern, the beauty of colours discerning the elements - the impression cannot match anything in the whole world. I have visited many museums, palaces, and watched lots of famous magazines and albums.

Why such a dream about the conversion of a stinky place?
Most probably to indicate the possibility of corporate achievement through the individuals when **they act how it feels right in their placement**.
Or, to support my controversial philosophy unpleasant to delicate ears, "the most beautiful flowers will grow on dung", meaning that noble deeds will shine better in areas polluted with corruption, crime and grime.
The boys must have followed inner guidance, intuition, inner knowing; trusted their God within.
The designer from above can only perform through dedicated individuals. To accomplish equals to begin. And then all the know-how secrets will be revealed through the mind of heart - the embassy of God's presence.

The POWER of your Will.

Whatever you are doing, never forget that God is on your side, the most powerful and most magnificent one; OMNIPRESENT, OMNIPOTENT, OMNISCIENT. If you are scared by any of your problems, if you magnify it over God - you give your evidence how silly you are, how foolish you are, how insane you are.

"Abide in Me, and I in you" – if you keep in mind such gospel tuition, it will serve as a condition that God can feel invited to influence your will, to guide you openly. Only then are you able to govern with authority over every set of circumstances - then your voice counts and you have the power to overcome any obstacle on the way; actually, you will see the dilemmas rushing away.

Remember that Jesus said, "I give you power over all the power of the enemy."
Pay attention as it sounds. This declaration is not about an everyday power over specific problems – this is YOUR POWER over ALL Powers causing your problems because Jesus knew that the enemy would raise obstructions, complications, barriers in generous quantity and quality.

In every case, you have the legal power to say, "No, I do not agree!"

If you sound with authority, if you are more than sure about your decision, any demons, disease, distress have to go away. The evil energy will recognise God's power active within you.

Whatever I write, I have already checked, or I am doing such commitments, declarations at the moment of writing about them. My latest victory is over notorious calls by marketing scammers about accidents, finances, other offers... In the last week, everyone switched off after hearing my one word "Hello".
Sometimes I could recognise the call from the same number - could be a different person at the job. Every time the same result. There cannot be such guideline for these marketers not to speak to a person who sounds confident – this must be reaction dictated by the inner spirit of the caller not to disturb a bold authority with their offer.

After some time longer, no scam calls at all.
It is good to be vigilant and understand why something is happening and then take full advantage of the experience, set up a defence – otherwise, the pattern will repeat itself in another occurrence.

By the Divine law, It's illegal for the demonic forces to trespass your will. Yet, you must know it and declare the power of your intention to maintain dominion over your body, home, life in your territory. You have to govern your universe with authority, with no trace of doubt.

If you are not overflowing with confidence, the enemy will keep close and will try to occupy any space again; step by step, starting with insertion of a little doubt first. Your heart will automatically tell you, will raise the alarm - but many people like to suppress such first feeling saying; honey, do not pose problems over tiny things.

Leave it for later, and it will usually be too late. To clear up the mess, it will take you a few days, and again, you will have to put aside something essential, something which could set barriers to the next sequence of problems.

Leave it to be, no point to raise the alarm over spilt milk, then look for the silver lining are the traits seeded in your mind by the enemy. Your optimism will seek for an open door; your enemy will open it for you with enticing vision at first, and then slowly delivering more agony while exploding with triumph over your destiny.

If you simultaneously prayed to God for help and blessed the problem, then left it to God to clear up the clutter – only then would you benefit from the wisdom of proverbial sayings!

You should agree with me that at an ancient time when proverbs arose and became the core of folk wisdom, it was the standard behaviour to get lost in prayers.

Without prayers, such golden statements enriched the enemy's arsenal of tools to manipulate you.

And in the meantime, your boundaries corrode slowly from outside, and soon you will even cease to exist inside, something will dilute your essence. It is happening all the time everywhere; step by step, step by Step, Step by Step... at a peaceful pace, quietly, not to awake your common sense, not to trigger the alarm of resistance.

In no time, invisibly, unintentionally, unknowingly you will surrender to the enemy; you will fulfil demons' dreams-come-true because you will always be in too much of inner turmoil to be able to set up your dreams.

Just now I received a Facebook request – on the latest Post I could read a few lines of the latest news in one sequence:
" Appeal launched to help family of young man stabbed to death in Rotherham
Crosses have been knocked over (on an area of open space on Church Street, where a war memorial stands) and graffiti has been daubed...

The vandalism attack came two days after Armistice Day, also known as Remembrance Day, which marks the day World War One ended...
LATEST: Man charged with attempted murder over stabbing of 16-year-old boy in Sheffield."

Who is doing that? Often teenagers with the written beast number over their hands or chest or forehead. I heard about it long ago, read in newspapers - nowadays it is not correct standard to mention such kind of absurd. In books by PhD Wanda Pratnicka, I learned that such a group, after vandalism on a local cemetery, once came to her home for help. When the teenagers came to their senses, they were terrified, claimed they had not known what they were doing; Wanda removed their evil spirits.

 Wanda wrote that more than often, many murderers she could see on TV news – were innocent personalities who acted on the inner demon's demands.
It may explain many cases when criminalist's neighbours are petrified saying – he was such a nice chap!

Wanda removed a ghost from me over the telephone in a few seconds – she can command and persuade the stuck spirit to leave to the Light. It was so easy because I called her in a few hours after sensing the problem.

I am a powerful Healer; I was acting in International Festivals. Often, from my home, I performed distant healing to many strangers or situations. To speed up the process of distant healing, I sometimes transferred the images of people into my heart. Very often, I was not strict about protection – once someone's ghost decided to stay in me.

Luckily, I had met Wanda just a few weeks earlier. I was under the impression of her book, freshly read, and I was able to recognise the problem and receive immediate help. At that period of my life, I did not believe in ghosts, and I was involved in New Age teachings.
I dread thinking who I would become until now.

In whichever state you are now, know that you are on the safest side when you are rooted in God. It is so easy, say only: Jesus, be my Lord. And have faith that He will never reject you, however little you seem to be, in terms of size and validity.

And He will diminish any errors about rules or procedure while you are presenting your request. Best if the wish is expressed directly from your heart. Be Bold to come to the Throne – runs through the whole Bible.

May God's invitation "Abide in Me and I in you" sounds like the sweetest lullaby, becomes the most active pulling magnetic force, better still - seek for the state of intimacy with God.
I will share later my personal experience; for now, for your sake, remember to practise advice as in the next Title: **"Be bold to approach and join and dwell in the Divine."**

The Image published from Facebook Post, with the consent of my Friend Fujio Noguchi.

ABOUT THE AUTHOR

At the age of 4 or 5, a tiny girl made a commitment to God that she would write books to change the world. Krystyna has kept that moment in her memory, being constantly aware of her broken promise.

 Now, as she gets closer to gates of ETERNITY, as a Granny, she decided to grab the pen. Krystyna decrees through gift of Prophecy and Dreams: *May these books find the way to every pair of hands to empower & lighten everyone's life.*
May they lead all humanity to heavenly Eternity.
- Come back my son to God, your real home -
Now, Krystyna has recovered from life-long lack of energy, memory loss and will proceed with writing... and will take care of her dormant Pages.

Follow me on FB:
https://www.facebook.com/krystyna.napierala.3

Like my Pages :
https://www.facebook.com/IAllowedMyselfToBe
https://www.facebook.com/33DreamsComeTrue/
https://www.facebook.com/Dreams-Come-True-148054345322187

Visit: www.london-angels-olympics.com
         http://healthyfood2loseweight.com/
Email: krynap369@gmail.com